Deer Isle's
UNDEFEATED
AMERICA'S CUP CREWS

—————————— ⚓ ——————————

HUMBLE HEROES FROM A DOWNEAST ISLAND

MARK J. GABRIELSON

Charleston H London

THE
History
PRESS

Published by The History Press
Charleston, SC 29403
www.historypress.net

Front cover: The Foul: America's Cup 1895 by Russ Kramer. www.russkramer.com.

First published 2013
Second printing 2013
Third printing 2013

Manufactured in the United States

ISBN 978.1.60949.728.6

Library of Congress CIP data applied for.

Notice: The information in this book is true and complete to the best of our knowledge. It is offered without guarantee on the part of the author or The History Press. The author and The History Press disclaim all liability in connection with the use of this book.

For Betsy

CONTENTS

ACKNOWLEDGEMENTS

In 2007, a group of Deer Isle–Stonington High School students began to sort out which of their ancestors had sailed aboard *Defender* and *Columbia*. Supported by Maine's CREST program (Community for Rural Education Stewardship and Technology), their teachers and local businessman and philanthropist William "Bill" Whitman, these high school students had a remarkable and enlightening year. Over the summer, seven of them made a trip to Valencia, Spain, to meet and see firsthand the graceful monohulls competing in the 2007 America's Cup series. Later in the year, nineteen students worked together to assemble genealogical and historical information that linked them and their families to their heroes of the late nineteenth century. The project culminated in a three-day trip that included visits to Newport, Rhode Island; the Herreshoff Museum in Bristol, Rhode Island; Mystic Seaport Museum and Archives in Mystic, Connecticut; and the New York Yacht Club in New York City. In New York, they were feted by author and noted sailor John Rousmaniere and other club notables. When this author visited these same places while researching this book, I could see tangible evidence that these students had contributed important information and artifacts to the repositories of these institutions on the 1895 and 1899 America's Cup defenses. They contributed their findings to the historical record. For that contribution and for the teachers who inspired and guided them, I am grateful.

Deer Isle is and was blessed with many who care about its history and legacy. Dr. Benjamin Noyes, a remarkable man who served as island general

The imposing home and office of Dr. Benjamin Noyes overlooked Stonington Harbor. Dr. Noyes cared deeply about his Deer Isle patients and was a meticulous genealogist and island historian. *Courtesy of the Penobscot Marine Museum, Searsport, Maine.*

practitioner from 1895 until his death in 1945, cared deeply about the genealogy of the island, and his records hold deep ancestral information, photographs and anecdotes about life on Deer Isle in the nineteenth and early twentieth centuries. His records are preserved and fully accessible at the Deer Isle–Stonington Historical Society (DISHS) on the island. Every small town should hope for a historical benefactor as conscientious as Dr. Noyes.

Tinker Crouch is the current president of the Deer Isle–Stonington Historical Society and an enthusiastic and helpful supporter of this project. Also at DISHS, Connie Wiberg, great-granddaughter of Charlie Scott, mastheadman on *Defender* and quartermaster aboard *Columbia*, opened all available island records and photographic collections to the author and added personal family anecdotes that were invaluable. Bill Whitman, who is a descendant of ancient Deer Isle families and also has an America's Cup sailor as an ancestor, gave direction and inspiration, particularly in the early phases. William Haviland, professor emeritus of anthropology at the University of Vermont and longtime resident of the island, has been a fount of knowledge on many of the more conspicuous Deer Isle sailors. His series on the yachting culture of Deer Isle at the turn of the century published in the local Deer Isle *AdVantages* newspaper is a cogent and invaluable source.

ACKNOWLEDGEMENTS

John Rousmaniere, accomplished author, speaker, sailor and expert on the America's Cup, was helpful from the beginning and throughout production. John gave early credence to the idea that focusing on the crews of the big cutters racing at the end of the nineteenth century might be a useful contribution to the history of this extraordinary event.

At the New York Yacht Club, Bill Whitman and John Rousmaniere paved the way to Vanessa Cameron's desk in the wonderful, dusty and venerable library at the clubhouse overlooking Forty-fourth Street in Manhattan. Vanessa retrieved difficult-to-access records of the 1895 and 1899 defenses, including original correspondence among Iselin, Herreshoff and Dunraven. The New York Yacht Club is one of this country's great private institutions, and their archives are a rich source of information on both yacht racing and high society in nineteenth- and early twentieth-century New York.

At Mystic Seaport, Maribeth Bielinski, Mary Anne Stets, Louisa Watrous and Carol Mowrey all provided extraordinary search, production and intellectual property support (over multiple author visits). Their help was essential as the author explored the vast and marvelous image archives in the Rosenfeld and Hope Goddard Iselin collections. They are genuinely interested in helping authors tell the stories of America's maritime heritage, and their diligence and encouragement are appreciated. Mystic Seaport holds among the most comprehensive and valuable photographic archives and artifact collections relating to American yachting, whaling and commercial shipping. It is also well organized and accessible to the researcher.

Kevin Johnson, photography curator at the Penobscot Marine Museum in Searsport, helped the author access the image archives at that gem of a museum in downeast Maine. The *American Fisherman* collection is vast, and Kevin was instrumental in selecting the images that give context to the Deer Isle sailormen and their origins.

Kurt Hasselbach and Nathan Burgess were doorways to the Hart Nautical Collections at MIT. The Hart collections contain essentially all known extant drawings from the Herreshoff Manufacturing Company. This work helped reveal the design similarities and differences among *Defender, Columbia* and *Reliance*.

John Palmieri and Noreen Rickson at the Rebecca Chase Library at the Herreshoff Museum in Bristol, Rhode Island, sourced clippings and photos of the *Defender* and *Columbia* series. The Herreshoff Museum is housed within several of the buildings remaining from the glory days of the Herreshoff yard and, along with the America's Cup Hall of Fame across the street, is well worth a visit.

Chuck Paine is a noted marine architect and designer of fast and comfortable cruising sailboats. Chuck gave the author a professional's perspective and made (literally) back-of-the-envelope calculations that helped unravel the facts of the *Defender* waterline controversy involving Lord Dunraven.

Finally, Whitney Tarella Landis, commissioning editor at The History Press, helped the author make sense of the writing and production processes. In addition to setting deadlines, without which no author could effectively produce any useable work, Whitney was encouraging, directive and demanding of accuracy and good writing. Hopefully her influence is evident.

The author takes full responsibility for the contents of this book. I know that there are errors here—I just don't know what they are. There are many writers and readers who are and will continue to be fascinated by the America's Cup, and I hope to hear from many of them to help fill out this story of the remarkable men from Deer Isle, Maine. This is a story that should be told and retold ever more clearly and accurately.

INTRODUCTION

Deer Isle, Maine produces two commodities in profusion. One is a sailorman, and the other is granite.[1]

In the winter of 1895, emissaries from the New York Yacht Club traveled more than 450 miles by train and steamboat to remote Deer Isle, Maine, to recruit the crew they needed to defend the America's Cup. At the time, the America's Cup yacht races were the most prestigious, widely followed and expensive international sporting events in the world. In 1899, the club sent word to the island that it needed yet another crew, and again Deer Isle sent their best sailing men to New York to defend the cup.

With so much at stake, why did the New York Yacht Club go all the way to Deer Isle to find a crew? The island may have been famous for its pink and purple granite, but how did they know about its fine sailors? Why did the emissaries bypass the dozens of coastal towns and islands along the New England coast that lie between New York and downeast Maine, many populated by hardworking and accomplished watermen? Why did they abandon the previously successful strategy of manning defense yachts with professionals drawn from a mix of Europeans to assemble an all-Yankee crew? And why were two defenses manned by Deer Islers in 1895 and 1899 but never again?

The America's Cup literature is vast but shallow. Excellent pictorial and literary work by Rosenfeld, Beken, Brooks, Lawson and, more recently, Rousmaniere, feature the boats, designers, skippers, sailing tactics, syndicates, clubs and even the lawyers who populate the remarkable sixteen-decade

Above: Penobscot Bay fishermen and their codfish catch photographed at the end of the nineteenth century. The Maine fishing business was and still is a family effort with multiple generations in partnership. *Courtesy of the Penobscot Marine Museum, Searsport, Maine.*

Left: William Elmer Hardy at age ninety. Hardy served as messboy aboard *Defender*. *Courtesy of the Deer Isle–Stonington Historical Society. Photograph by the author.*

Opposite: The crew bending on the mainsail aboard *Columbia* in Bristol, Rhode Island, July 1899. *Image © Mystic Seaport, #1951.14.10.*

history of the America's Cup. Larger-than-life people like Hank Haff, Charlie Barr, J.P. Morgan, Nathanael Herreshoff, Harold Vanderbilt, Ted Turner, Dennis Conner, Sir Peter Blake, Tom Schnackenberg, Larry Ellison, Brad Butterworth, Ernesto Bertarelli, Sir Russell Coutts, Olin and Rod Stephens, William Fife and perhaps the most celebrated of all, Sir Thomas Lipton, live in this literature.

What is missing are the stories of the crews—the individuals and teams who sailed the boats. The literature written about the 1895 and 1899 defenses doesn't mention George Conant, Fred Weed, Win Conary, Coo Eaton, Montie and Spunk Haskell, Willie Pickering or Will Hardy. It misses the heroics of Charlie Scott and the perspective of Ed Wood. These were important men in the cup races and the controversies and dramas that surrounded these events. Particularly in the early days, including the 1890s, these were the people who not only sailed the yachts but also assembled standing rigging, bent the sails on, handled the running rigging, risked their necks aloft or on bowsprits awash, maintained the boats and even cooked and laundered for their teammates at dock. They were the subject of rules, regulation and controversy. They also knew the truth about the shadier sides of high-level international sailboat racing.

Boats have met to race for the America's Cup races thirty-four times from 1851 through 2010. The thirty-fifth series will be held in 2013 in San Francisco. In all of those years, not one book has been dedicated to telling the story of the crews—where they came from, who they were and what made them such great sailors.

The Deer Isle crews of 1895 and 1899 are the most interesting of all. They were courageous, skilled, accomplished, dedicated, sometimes disagreeable and altogether human. They were loyal and surprisingly sophisticated. Perhaps most importantly, they were effective as a team. Since they all knew each other, having grown up together in a small Maine island community, this group of sailors could meld into a racing team in a very short period of time. They were asked to give, and they gave a lot. They were also undefeated.

This book will show that once the New York Yacht Club syndicates decided to recruit all-American crews, it *had* to go to Deer Isle, Maine. The nation's sporting yachtsmen knew that great sailors lived and worked there. Deer Isle sailors had a well-established reputation as competent, reliable and affordable sail handlers and yachting officers. It is true that many were or had been farmers and sailing fishermen, but Deer Isle men were in wide circulation as big yacht crewmen and commanders. If they weren't yachting, they could be found working on merchant vessels owned by their Deer Isle or Penobscot Bay neighbors. Typically, these were modestly successful coastal shippers who frequently called at Boston, New Haven, New York and often well beyond.

The Deer Isle America's Cup crews were not rural hicks. They were humble and hardworking Americans. They also recognized a good deal when they saw one. The New Yorkers paid well, and when compared to the typically difficult life a Deer Isle man led at sea or ashore, the work was pleasant. Sailing a big, new and fast yacht off Sandy Hook, New Jersey, on a balmy summer's day was light duty when contrasted with hauling traps in a cold, blustery downeast dawn or handling frozen ropes aboard a schooner loaded to the gunwales with lumber or granite as it flailed its way up west to Boston through dirty weather. What happened on Deer Isle in 1895 and 1899 is remarkable, but it also is understandable.

A relaxed *Columbia* crew. *Courtesy of the Deer Isle–Stonington Historical Society.*

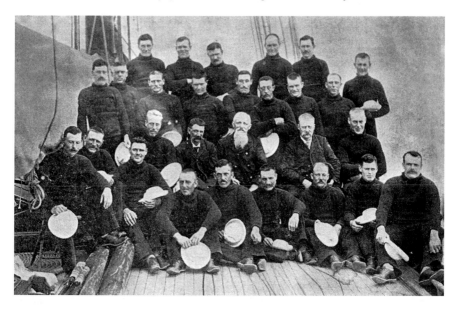

The *Defender* crew. Hank Haff is in the center sporting his trademark white beard. *Courtesy of the Deer Isle–Stonington Historical Society.*

Never before and never since has one town provided the entire American muster for the America's Cup. Deer Isle did it twice. The 1895 and 1899 victorious America's Cup defense crews were arguably (and still remain) among the best large-boat competitive sailing teams ever assembled.

Chapter 1

ORIGINS AND EARLY HISTORY OF THE AMERICA'S CUP

When they shipped aboard *Defender* in 1895, the first Deer Isle crew was joining an event that had already been raced ten times over the preceding fifty-five years. The schooner *America* had won a single race around the Isle of Wight off England's southern coast in 1851. For nearly twenty years, nothing happened as the New Yorkers thought about what to do with the trophy and the United States fought bitterly over what to do with itself as a nation. With the Civil War over, the first challenge came across the sea in 1870. After that, the challenges came thick and fast, sometimes once each sailing season. The New York Yacht Club was particularly busy in the 1880s, beating back four challengers over ten years. The enchantment with yachting was sustained even as the nation suffered through the stock market panic of 1893, the worst economic downturn since the founding of the country and until the Great Depression. Yachting on both shores of the Atlantic was experiencing its heyday. The United States was a rapidly growing but just emerging maritime power, but its high society was taking the sport of sailing very seriously. Great Britain, on the other hand, was at its naval and merchant marine apogee. Great Britain was the undisputed ruler of the waves and considered herself mistress royal of yacht racing as well. By the turn of the century, the United States merchant fleet had 1.3 million tons under sail—but the British had 2.9 million. The American steamship fleet was rated at 811 thousand tons, while Great Britain had 11 million tons steaming under its flag—more than ten times the weight of the Americans.

A fanciful 1895 cartoon showing a British gentleman pursuing the elusive cup from the *New York Herald*. The *Herald* and other papers from London, Glasgow, New York, Boston and elsewhere followed the America's Cup races closely. *Courtesy of the New York Yacht Club.*

Despite their power, competence and tradition, the British were unable to win those yacht races off New York's coast. Great Britain's inability to win back the cup must have been terribly frustrating and provocative. The Deer Isle crews came down from Maine to join an intense, costly and enormously popular competition that was propelled by personal, social and even national emotional currents.

The Yacht *America*, 1851

In February 1851, the commodore of the Royal Yacht Squadron (RYS) in Cowes, on the Isle of Wight in England, wrote a letter to John Cox Stevens, a founder and then commodore of the five-year-old New York Yacht Club. In the letter, the Earl of Wilton confessed knowledge that the Americans were interested in campaigning a yacht in England the following summer. Wilton also knew that Stevens and his colleagues were having a new schooner built for the purpose. The RYS commodore invited the New Yorkers to come to Cowes to participate in a few races and enjoy use of the squadron's clubhouse, a generous invitation considering the Royal Yacht Squadron was among England's most venerable and oldest yacht clubs.

However, generosity and civility were not all that motivated Wilton's invitation. The English gentleman of the Victorian age was an enthusiastic sportsman, and he was also a betting man. Yachtsmen did not simply race for trophies; they raced for wagers as well. International competitive sailing was widening and deepening betting pockets. The New York Yacht Club syndicate was well aware of the English sport-betting scene. They were building a new schooner that the members hoped would more than pay for itself not just in glory but also financial return.

The schooner the club had commissioned was designed by George Steers, a brilliant young engineer who had already designed a number of successful racing schooners. Christened *America*, the new yacht was a descendant of the Sandy Hook pilot boats that met ships arriving in New York Harbor. Seaworthy and fast, Sandy Hook pilot designs were driven by the economic need to deliver pilots to ships reliably and efficiently. Steers had been hired by a syndicate of club members consisting of Commodore Stevens, his brother Edwin, Hamilton Wilkes, J. Beekman Finlay and George Schuyler. *America* slid down the ways at the William Brown Shipyard on the East River in downtown Manhattan in May 1851, dangerously late for the summer race season across the Atlantic in England. It began hurried sea trials and in the course of those trials broke its foremast. A new one was installed, and the riggers added shroud bumpkins to widen the purchase of the foremast rigging onto the narrow fore section of the yacht. The improvement worked, and *America* was ready for sea and a season of racing.

At just over ninety-three feet overall, with a clipper bow, a broad beam aft and raked masts, *America* was a large yacht for the time. It also was very different from the English standard against which it would race. The British yachts were bluff-bowed, beamier forward and narrow aft, and they rather resembled a dolphin fish. The English designs were derived from centuries of trial. *America*'s lines were derived from trial and modern engineering. *America*'s sails, made by Colt's in Patterson, New Jersey, were constructed from American cotton duck cloth. They were conspicuously less baggy than those of the European rivals, as the British yachts used heavier sailcloth, typically made from hemp. In many ways, *America* was a departure from tradition—a product of the new world and the engineering innovations arising from it.

Stevens and the New York Yacht Club syndicate took ownership of *America* in June 1851. Later that month, with thirteen men aboard, *America* departed New York for England. Its captain was Dick Brown, a New York Harbor pilot. Designer George Steers was aboard, as were his brother James Steers and James's young son. Records at the New York Customs House show that of the thirteen men who sailed *America* across the Atlantic, six sailed "before the mast" as ordinary seamen. We know nothing about these six men. In all likelihood, they were composed of crewmen from Steven's and Schuyler's yachts, as well as, perhaps, riggers and workmen from the Brown shipyard brought along for their tradesman's skills as well as their sailing abilities.

America was the first American yacht to cross the Atlantic Ocean to race in England on its own bottom. The passage across the ocean also was its shakedown sail, albeit under a cut-down pilot rig. Steers and Stevens anticipated that they would learn some new things about the yacht on the trip, both in rig and hull, that if corrected would make *America* more competitive. They chose Le Havre, France, as their landfall. *America* reached Le Havre in just over twenty days, a fast passage.

Stevens had the yacht hauled out of the water, and the French yard workers and American crewmen made alterations to its bow and installed a taller yacht-racing rig. *America*'s owners were also already at the game. If *America* was to be successful, it had to appear in British waters with its features largely unknown. Stevens wanted to come up on the British fleet with *America* still a mystery. His intention was to make the racing (and betting) as interesting as possible.

America arrived in the Solent off of Cowes at the end of July 1851, newly painted and fully outfitted for the racing season in England. As it approached the Isle of Wight, it was boarded by an English pilot, Captain Edward Stephens, from the pilot vessel *Ibis*. Due to light winds, its captain, Dick Brown, had decided to anchor well off the harbor to await the dawn and, hopefully, a freshening breeze. Despite the gentle breeze, Edwards developed an impression of *America*'s potential speed, later describing it as a "regular flying fish" to the English papers. *America*'s speed was proving difficult to hide.

The following morning, in a six-knot wind, the British racing cutter *Lavrock* came out to welcome *America* to Cowes. Stevens later admitted that the urge to race, to get a fix on *America*'s speed compared to a British flyer, proved irresistible. Although laden with heavy transatlantic provisions and gear, *America* easily sailed past *Lavrock* and arrived in Cowes anchorage a quarter of a mile ahead. Thus, in its first (albeit informal) race, *America* handily beat an acknowledged British racing yacht.

The unfortunate consequence of this display made it difficult for *America* to find willing racing opponents. The venture to England was at risk of becoming a failure for the Americans—not because their new yacht was too slow but because it was too fast. Finally, Stevens wrote the Royal Yacht Squadron a letter requesting entry in the club's annual regatta race around the Isle of Wight. The RYS magnanimously agreed to allow the *America* entry, and on August 22, 1851, in perhaps the most famous yacht race of all time, *America* out-sailed a fleet of eighteen British yachts on the fifty-three-mile circumnavigation of the island. It handily won what newspapers on both sides of the Atlantic called the "World's Regatta."

America did not return to home waters until much later. Shortly after its dramatic victory, its businessmen owners sold it to Lord John de Blaquiere for £5,000. *America* remained in Britain until it reappeared in Savannah, Georgia, in 1861 under the ownership of Henry Decie, an English yachtsman probably sympathetic to the Confederacy. It was brought into the Confederate navy under the name *Memphis.* When it was evading capture by Federal forces while running the Federal blockade, *Memphis* (nee *America*) was deliberately scuttled in Florida's St. Johns River.

After the war, *America* was found by Federal lieutenant John Stevens (no relation to *America*'s original owner). It was raised, repaired and commissioned into the U.S. Navy as a training ship. With its original name restored to its transom, it reappeared in the first Challenge Cup races organized by the New York Yacht Club after the Civil War ended. In 1870, the British challenger *Cambria* raced against a fleet of seventeen New York Yacht Club yachts, and largely for sentimental reasons, *America* was entered in the regatta. Sailed by Navy midshipmen, it was under the command of the son of Dick Brown, its skipper when it won off Cowes in 1851. It finished fourth overall, behind the American winner *Magic* but well ahead of the British challenger *Cambria*. *America* was eventually broken up in 1941 when the shed in which it was stored collapsed under a load of snow.

Apart from pride, a little publicity and the proceeds from the sale of their yacht, *America*'s owners returned to the United States in 1851 with little to show for their victory. They had won only short money in the scarce wagering they had managed to arrange. The trophy *America* had claimed was an odd-looking and overly ornate ewer, commissioned earlier in the year to Gerard's silversmiths of London as the 1851 RYS regatta prize. Called the Queen's Cup, it was an ordinary trophy commissioned for an ordinary year of racing. It was homely and of modest value. However, this silver-plated trophy was to become the most sought-after spoil of victory in sport. It became so only after the *America* syndicate, and the New York Yacht Club, through what later proved to be brilliant publicity and myth-making (some planned and some unintentional), transformed the Queen's Cup into the America's Cup, with all of its connotations and symbolism.

THE DEED OF GIFT

Apart from winning the Isle of Wight circumnavigation, the earliest block in the foundation underpinning the America's Cup myth was the original "Deed of Gift." Drafted by four of the five *America* owners—John and Edwin Stevens, George Schuyler and J. Beekman Finlay (Colonel Hamilton Wilkes was unable to participate as he was ill abroad)—the Deed of Gift was a letter conjoined to the trophy when the syndicate decided to give it to the New York Yacht Club. The syndicate recognized that the unique circumstances under which the trophy had been gained was a compelling and long-term concept. It could be portrayed as, and in fact, occasionally proved to be, sportsmanship of the highest order. Based on their direct experience in both England and the United States, such an event would attract newspaper coverage and the intrigue of the social elite. In short, arranging such a sporting event would help the fledgling New York Yacht Club achieve the status its founding membership coveted.

Originally drafted and later reinterpreted and clarified by George Schuyler, the Deed of Gift and trophy were finally presented to the club on July 8, 1857. The original Deed of Gift is a short document. It confined the envisioned contest to one among any "organized Yacht Club." Individuals were expressly excluded from challenging or defending the trophy (which became important in deflecting the first challenge received, which came immediately after the Civil War). To eliminate any doubt, the original Deed of Gift states that the "cup is to be the property of the club," not any club's members or owners of the yachts that win it. The *America* syndicate was most concerned with the future of the New York Yacht Club, as opposed to the gain of fame and fortune (or loss of it, as the case might have been) for themselves.

The original deed was nearly silent on the rules of racing, as the rules of engagement once a challenge had been received and accepted were to be worked out between the competing clubs. *America* had raced at a time of high Corinthian sportsmanship—a time when honor and a spirit of fair play seemed to dominate the more modern relentless pursuit of victory. It was the sincere hope of the syndicate that yacht clubs could and would amicably reach agreement over the rules and regulations governing the races, including the origins and characteristics of skippers, officers and crews. That idealistic notion of amicability proved to be short-lived.

THE EARLY CHALLENGES AND DEFENSES

The first challenge addressed to the New Yorkers came from Englishman James Ashbury, heir to a Manchester fortune (which he would later lose) made by his father building railway cars. Ashbury suffered from respiratory disease (probably asthma), and in order to improve his health, he moved to Brighton on England's southern shore. To improve his social standing, he took up yachting. He rose to commodore of the Royal Harwich Yacht Club. His first challenge for the cup was expressed through his magnificent ocean racer *Cambria*, which in the summer of 1870 soundly defeated the American schooner *Dauntless* in an east to west transatlantic race. Organizing the race against *Dauntless* had given Ashbury an excuse to bring *Cambria* to New York in spite of his protracted and sometimes unanswered correspondence with the New York Yacht Club concerning a challenge for the "America's Queens Cup." *Cambria* raced against fifteen American schooners, most of which had centerboards, or "movable keels" as the British called them. Centerboards were considered unseaworthy by Ashbury and his countrymen and were therefore explicitly forbidden by the British in their home races. In the single race held on August 8, 1870, on the New York Yacht Club "inner course" off Sandy Hook and along the southern coast of Long Island, *Cambria* followed seven American boats across the finish line, but with its time corrected under a pre-agreed handicap system (itself a topic of great controversy) was awarded tenth place. The sentimental *America* finished fourth, and the overall winner was the schooner *Magic*, owned by Franklin Osgood.

The crews of all of these vessels were professionals hired for the racing season. *Cambria* had just completed its transatlantic defeat of *Dauntless*, so its crew was hardened and experienced with the boat. Although no crew musters survive, the American boats, *Magic* included, were crewed by picked hands accustomed to sailing for their owners in the summer racing circuits off of New York, Oyster Bay, Larchmont and Newport, the prime yacht-racing venues of the era. Some may have hailed from Deer Isle, although no record remains of these individual crewmen. These were professionals who knew their yachts well. The New York Yacht Club had not yet developed the event to the point where purpose-built yachts and purpose-built crews were required.

Almost immediately upon his return to England, Ashbury revived a correspondence with the New York Yacht Club. Not satisfied that his challenger should cross the Atlantic to race against a fleet of the best in the New York Yacht Squadron, Ashbury insisted that the "match" concept conveyed by the Deed of Gift was not one against a fleet but one against one. The New York Yacht Club deferred to George Schuyler, the sole surviving member of the *America* syndicate. Schuyler found in favor of Ashbury. With remarkable foresight or perhaps sensibility regarding what constituted fair play and good sportsmanship, Schuyler opined that a match should, in fact, be a one-on-one race or series of races. Despite the fact that *America* had sailed across the Atlantic, had raced against the combined best of the Royal Yacht Squadron and had not provided a fair financial return on its owner's investment, Schuyler in effect modified the rules of this international sporting event. He thereby improved its stature as a fair test of yachting prowess and increased its interest among sailors, the media and, of course, the news-reading public.

Ashbury had commissioned an enormous schooner, the *Livonia*, specifically for the purpose of retaking the cup. *Livonia* was 126 feet overall, 107 on the waterline and spread over 18,000 square feet of canvas. It arrived in New York on October 1, 1871, after a difficult passage that included damage to a mast and bowsprit. Over the next few weeks, *Livonia* raced three times against the New York Yacht Club's finest; first against an early *Columbia*, and twice against *Sappho*. In the first race, *Columbia* won in light air. In the second, which was sailed two days later in a near gale, *Columbia* won again, but the victory was protested by Ashbury. When asked by *Columbia*'s captain, the race committee had informed him that the windward stake boat could be left either to port or starboard. No one thought to inform the *Livonia* afterguard of the optionality. In Britain, it was customary to always leave the stake boat to starboard. In this event, *Columbia* rounded the mark, leaving it to port as part of an elegant jibe. Not knowing that a portside rounding was an option, and in its effort to leave the mark to starboard, *Livonia* placed itself at a significant disadvantage. It went on to lose the race.

The *Dauntless* was scheduled to defend in the third race but was damaged while under tow. America's Cup historian Jerome Brooks noted that after *Dauntless* had been incapacitated, "the *Columbia* was hastily drafted, though her captain had been partly disabled through an accident and her crew was recovering from a night's victory celebration."[2] This was not the last time that an America's Cup defense crew was overtaxed by New York's recreational opportunities.

Columbia proceeded to lose the third race. It was a light-weather boat, which was precisely the reason that the New York Yacht Club had attempted the switch to *Dauntless*. *Sappho* was selected to race in the next two and defeated *Livonia* in both. With victories in four out of five races, the Americans retained the cup, although the series was marked by controversy and some ill will, preludes to the discomforts of the defenses to follow.

The next challenge came in 1876 from Canada, considered an unlikely source. The Americans had always assumed challenges would arise from England. After all, the United States and Great Britain were the undisputed lions of competitive yacht racing. Major Charles Gifford of the Royal Canadian Yacht Club of Toronto thought otherwise. He had had a schooner, the *Countess of Dufferin*, designed and built by Alexander Cuthbert. It barely made it to New York, Colonel Gifford having nearly run out of money as she neared completion at Cuthbert's yard. For the first time, the New York Yacht club had agreed to field only one boat rather than selecting a defender *du jour* from its fleet depending on weather conditions or, as in the case of *Columbia* five years before, the condition of the crew. However, despite the accomplishment of avoiding its owner's creditors and the single-vessel defense format, *Countess* lost to the New Yorkers' *Madeleine* in two straight races, the third of the three-race series being unnecessary.

In 1881, Cuthbert himself challenged again, this time with his own boat, the *Atalanta*. It was by far the smallest America's Cup boat to date and would retain that distinction until the twelve-meter era began in the late 1950s. Only seventy feet overall, it was less than half the length of Herreshoff's 1903 enormous masterpiece *Reliance*. *Atalanta* was badly out-sailed and beaten by the New York Yacht Club defender *Mischief*. In addition to its lopsidedness, this series was unique in several respects. First, the boats used balloon spinnakers for the first time. Second, Cuthbert was the only skipper in America's Cup history to design, build and skipper a challenger. Third, after Cuthbert suggested that he might challenge again after his poor performance, the New York Yacht Club hastily asked George Schuyler to redraft the Deed of Gift to make that eventuality an impossibility. The club was concerned that the level of competition was declining and that the cup might evolve into a North American event rather than a truly international one. Schuyler complied and added several provisions, including the rules that the challenger club must run their races on salt water and that a losing boat may not challenge again for at least two years. Finally, *Atalanta* was sailed largely by amateurs. It was soundly beaten by the professionals aboard *Mischief*, many of whom hailed from Scandinavia.

The 1880s was an extraordinarily busy decade in America's Cup history. The Americans were challenged in three sequential years: 1885, '86 and '87. Two separate British challenges arose in 1885, one from Sir Richard Sutton with *Genesta*, a new narrow-beamed and enormously successful racer, and the other from Lieutenant William Henn of the Royal Navy (retired) with *Galatea*. The New York Yacht Club deftly handled this embarrassment of riches by accepting the Sutton challenge and cordially deferring Henn's until the following racing season.

The 1885 American defense boat was *Puritan*, unique in both design and origin. It was the brainchild of the young and soon-to-be-proven brilliant designer Edward Burgess, and it hailed from Eastern Yacht Club in Boston. The New Yorkers recognized its speed, and by virtue of the fact that one of the *Puritan* syndicate members was also a member of the NYYC, were legitimately able to offer *Puritan* as the defender. The vessel proceeded to sweep *Genesta* in the first two races out of a best-of-three series.

The following year, 1886, saw the arrival of Lieutenant Henn's *Galatea*. A new boat from Edward Burgess, the *Mayflower*, soundly defeated this challenge as well. *Galatea* was a well-founded Edwardian-era yacht complete with Asian carpets and a pet monkey aboard. Heavy and seaworthy, it was no match for the lighter *Mayflower* in the light and drizzly airs it wallowed through off Sandy Hook.

In 1887, *Volunteer*, another Burgess design, defeated *Thistle* in a challenge brought by the Royal Clyde Yacht Club of Scotland. *Thistle* was designed by George Watson, who is considered to be one of the earliest yacht designers to use advanced engineering and scientific techniques. In this regard, Watson was a predecessor of the most successful yacht designer of all—Nathanael Herreshoff. In this series, Captain Henry "Hank" Haff made his America's Cup skippering debut. Haff had developed a reputation as an aggressive yacht-racing competitor and had broken in to the America's Cup scene the year prior as first officer aboard *Mayflower*. As we shall see later, it was Hank Haff's decision in 1895 to recruit an all-Deer Isle crew to man *Defender*, who then helped him win his most famous races. *Thistle* was skippered by John Barr, brother of Charles "Charlie" Barr, the Scottish-American immigrant whom we will meet later. In contrast to his brother, who sailed for Scotland and was criticized for his lackluster handling of *Thistle*, the younger Charlie developed into the giant of American yacht racing who early in his unequalled yacht-racing career skippered the all-Deer Isle manned *Columbia* in 1899. However, after that campaign, Charlie would never again command a Deer Isler. We shall see why.

The *Vigilant-Valkyrie II* races in 1893 ushered in two legends—one famous and the other infamous. *Vigilant* was the first of many of Nathanael Herreshoff's America's Cup defense designs. *Valkyrie II* was owned by the Fourth Earl of Dunraven, a nobleman, sportsman, politician and complete failure at public relations. Dunraven would challenge again in 1895 with *Valkyrie III* and would dominate yachting and sporting headlines for the wrong reasons. In the 1893 races, however, *Valkyrie II* proved to be a worthy challenger, probably matching *Vigilant* in boat speed in the heavy wind conditions that characterized their races. In one of the very few instances of recognizing the men at work on the boats, early America's Cup historian Jerome Brooks pointed to the skill of the *Vigilant* crew as perhaps the reason why *Vigilant* was able to defeat *Valkyrie II* in three straight races. In one of the more memorable passages in his book, Brooks wrote:

> *A 15-knot wind out of the east had a feel of much more to come. Crews and afterguards prepared for a wet race. A few minutes before the time for starting, the Valkyrie carried away part of a throat-halyard block. Captain Cranfield himself followed two men aloft to look at the nuisance. The main came down, and the block was replaced. On the Vigilant, the lifts couldn't get the centerboard down. These minor annoyances suggested that this was the right day for trouble. The Valkyrie's ability to point put her almost two minutes ahead at the outer mark. On the Vigilant, then about 600 yards astern, the situation called for some quick action. Up went her spinnaker. Then her balloon jib topsail was sent up in stops. Its halyard jammed in a hank. A hand scrambled to the topmast head and down its stay to release the fouled line. Two others went aloft, one to the sky at the topmast head, where he lashed the head and tack of the working topsail and prepared to send its halyard to the deck. His partner, hanging onto the wind with his teeth, hauled himself out on the gaff to help with the topsail and bring its sheet to deck.*
>
> *While these seagoing monkeys were working aloft—they were up there for a quarter of an hour and more—another hardy character…had gone out on the boom. That spar was then almost athwart the beam, and every so often, it sliced the crest off a wave. They tried to make it easy for the man by slinging him from the masthead in the bight of a gauntline and then dragging him along the boom with an outhaul. His orders were simple and direct: shake out the reef; if the points a' jammed cut them, and don't annoy us of that slippery round boom—you're wet enough right now. When the job was completed…the mainsail was swayed up full. The balloon jib topsail had been broken out, and then a small club topsail, already aloft, was tied in to windward of the lashing working sail.*

Deer Isle crewmen walking out on *Columbia*'s enormous round boom to prepare a reef. In the 1890s, America's Cup crewmen were commonly in the rigging taking calculated risks. *Image © Mystic Seaport, #1951.14.54.*

Yachting history has no record of such operations as those which had been performed on the Vigilant in that gale of wind. As a consequence of heroic efforts which had increased her sail spread, the defender leaped forward. The Vigilant came tearing on—and shot across the line...ahead of the challenger. It was, said the reporter of the New York Times, "probably the greatest battle of sails that was ever fought." Just who the men were—Norwegians, Swedes, Americans—whose deeds on the Vigilant were so valiant seems now to be forgotten.[3]

Among the Americans were a few Deer Islers. We know that Captain George Conant was second mate on five defenders: *Mayflower, Vigilant, Volunteer, Defender*

Nathanael Herreshoff (pointing) in Bristol, June 1895. Herreshoff was the most successful sailing yacht designer and builder of his age. The other gentleman and boy are unidentified. *Image © Mystic Seaport, #1951.15.3.*

and *Columbia.* He was a loyal friend to Captain Hank Haff and would later introduce Haff to many Deer Islers. Although Haff wasn't skippering *Vigilant* that day (Captain William Hansen was), the Deer Isle reputation as a nursery of great yachting sailors had been established, and Conant was aboard. We can't know for sure, but perhaps one or two of the heroes up in the *Vigilant* rigging on that blustery day, winners of the greatest downwind race leg in America's Cup history, came from Deer Isle, Maine.

Chapter 2

DEER ISLE, MAINE, AND WIVENHOE, ENGLAND, IN THE 1890S

DEER ISLE AND ITS EARLY SETTLEMENT

Deer Isle is one of the larger islands along the coast of Maine. Like Mount Desert Island to its east, Deer Isle hangs from the crenellated Maine coastline like an ornament from the branch of a spruce tree. Since 1939, it has dangled from the end of a graceful suspension bridge. According to islanders even today, the bridge opening was an event that "altered the soul" of Deer Isle, and not necessarily for the better.

When or why people started using the term "isle" to describe this downeast Maine island is unclear. The definitive family history of early Deer Isle was written by George L. Hosmer, a local genealogist and amateur historian. In the book, first published in 1886, Hosmer referred to the municipality as "Deer Isle" but the geographical feature it rested on as "Great Deer Island." Today, both town and island are referred to as Deer Isle. What the maps show today as Little Deer Isle, a small island (and individualistic neighborhood) connected to the larger Deer Isle by a stonework causeway, Hosmer called "Little Deer Island." To confuse matters even more, in Hosmer's day, the town of Deer Isle encompassed what is now three towns: the Town of Deer Isle (consisting of roughly the northern two thirds of the larger island plus Little Deer), Stonington (the southern third of the island and since 1897 a separate town) and Isle au Haut, a mid-sized island several miles to the south of Stonington, now also its own municipality. There is also a basket-full of stunningly beautiful small islands, some inhabited by humans, others only by spruce trees and wildlife, scattered

Deer Isle-Sedgwick Bridge under construction in 1938. *Courtesy of the Penobscot Marine Museum, Searsport, Maine.*

The opening of the Deer Isle-Sedgwick Bridge in 1939. The opening of the bridge connected Little Deer Isle to the mainland and for some residents "changed the soul" of the Deer Isle community. *Courtesy of the Penobscot Marine Museum, Searsport, Maine.*

Stonington Harbor at a low tide at the end of the nineteenth century. Tides in mid-coast Maine rise and fall ten to twelve feet, posing significant navigation challenges for sailors and fishermen. *Courtesy of the Penobscot Marine Museum, Searsport, Maine.*

Fishing smacks and dories in Stonington Harbor in the early 1900s. *Courtesy of the Penobscot Marine Museum, Searsport, Maine.*

around these three larger islands. These islands are severally parsed to the towns of Deer Isle, Stonington and Isle au Haut. The entire area is a cartographer's challenge but a sailor's delight.

The earliest European explorers and cartographers in the area were French, and to the surveyors go the honors of naming the places. Samuel Champlain sailed into Penobscot Bay in 1604, of which Deer Isle forms much of the eastern shoreline. He bestowed names on many prominent islands and features while there and drew the earliest European charts.

Prior to Champlain's visits, the lands and waters of Penobscot Bay were home to or seasonally visited by Native Americans. It is true that in many places, particularly in the names of rivers, bays, reaches and mountains, the Native American names have stuck. For example, near Deer Isle are Eggemoggin Reach, Penobscot Bay, the Kennebec and Sheepscot Rivers and Mount Megunticook. However, since the Europeans arrived, the Native Americans were forced to give way to French, British, Dutch, British Canadian and French Canadian conquerors and settlers. In certain places, the English names have taken permanent hold, particularly those assigned to towns and islands to the west of Deer Isle—places like Camden, Belfast and George's Island. Nearby, and particularly east of Deer Isle, the French names are more common. Here the maps show Isle au Haut, Mount Desert Island, Champlain Mountain, St. Sauveur Mountain and even Frenchman's Bay. The Dutch were least successful in naming features around Deer Isle, but after all, they were in charge of the region for the briefest period of time.

The European settlement history of Deer Isle begins in the mid-1700s, when an irresistible wave of land-hungry white settlers, primarily of English and Irish descent, radiated out from the crowding Massachusetts Bay colonies. The wave reached Deer Isle in the 1760s, when white families began crossing Eggemoggin Reach and clearing farmland on the northern shores of the large island. By the 1760s, about one hundred settlers and their dependants lived on the island. The Native Americans, who had descended the rivers on a seasonal basis to harvest the fish and shellfish resources of the island, building up massive piles of cast-off mollusk shells as evidence of their centuries of success, came less and less often. There is no evidence of direct violence between Native Americans and the European American settlers on Deer Isle, but like elsewhere, a well-armed European society with entrenched ideas of land ownership and property rights permanently displaced a migratory hunter-gatherer culture that viewed the islands and surrounding waters as resources to be exploited by all.

A horse-drawn carriage crossing the bar from Stinson Neck to Sunshine on Deer Isle. Before causeways were built to link the several islands that compose Deer Isle, travelers had to await low tide to make their way. *Courtesy of Penobscot Marine Museum, Searsport, Maine.*

By 1769, the Deer Isle settlement had reached such a level of prosperity and cohesiveness that the residents were preparing a petition to the Massachusetts colonial government to incorporate as a town. However, they were probably delayed in their ambitions by the increasing tensions between Maine's independence-minded residents and the British governor. As Edwin A. Churchill wrote:

> *The people in eastern Maine had their own particular problem. The dozen or so communities east of the Penobscot were denied legal incorporation by the Crown unless they renounced the right to send representatives to the Massachusetts General Court, a body the King felt was trouble enough without adding any more rebellious deputies. They refused and remained unincorporated. Thus, they could not validate their land titles or elect constables to control local rowdies.*[4]

Then came revolution. Deer Isle and its inhabitants were active in the American war for independence. Maine historian James Leamon wrote of an event that took place in the town of Naskeag, on the mainland side of Eggemoggin Reach:

> *In late July 1778, two British armed sloops* [warships of less than twenty guns each] *suddenly appeared, one of them commanded by Charles Callahan, a Tory refugee from Pownalborough. A landing party of sixty men easily brushed away the several defenders, burned their homes and barns, and then either carried off or destroyed the livestock. After exchanging some prisoners, the raiders continued their way up Eggemoggin Reach, plundering settlements and seizing fishing craft as they went. Isolated Naskeag received no military support until assistance arrived from Deer Isle the day after the raid.*[5]

As in other communities on the Maine coast, British raids and the general disruption of commerce caused severe hardship on Deer Isle during the Revolution. Deer Isle had to receive aid directly from the Provincial Congress in Boston. Leamon wrote:

> *Occasionally, the government offered aid directly, as when it voted to supply Deer Isle and Frenchman's Bay with pork, beef, molasses, and rice and to take their lumber in payment. To Deer Isle, the state also sent fishing gear to replace what had been lost and worn out.*[6]

The women suffered too, but they fought back. Leamon and Hutchinson tell the story of Mary Campbell, who successfully sued and recovered damages from an American privateer-turned-pirate who had sacked the Campbell house, which was located on the Deer Isle shore of Eggemoggin Reach (near present-day Campbell Island).[7]

The suffering experienced by Deer Islers during the Revolutionary War, as well as the War of 1812, during which the Penobscot Bay region was once again the scene of British raiding and naval destruction, instilled in the islanders a deep distrust of the British. Deer Isle sent a number of their own Tory families packing, most notably the Greenlaws. Perhaps these patriotic experiences foreshadowed the later Deer Islers' eagerness to crew aboard *Defender* in 1895 to protect the America's Cup from the British and again in 1899 aboard *Columbia* against the jovial but Irish-British Sir Thomas Lipton.

Deer Isle's incorporation had to wait until 1789, when hostilities with Great Britain had passed and normalcy had returned to the process of establishing communities in New England. When Deer Isle finally incorporated, the matter of land titles was foremost in everyone's mind. The matter was resolved, just as it was in many New England towns, with the establishment of a class of settler to whom land titles would be granted. On Deer Isle, these "proprietor" families were those who had settled on or before January 1, 1784. Each was granted title to one hundred acres in exchange for the cost of surveying the land and filing the deeds. Of the eighty Deer Islers who crewed on *Defender* or *Columbia* (and both in fourteen cases), sixty-six were descended from Deer Isle's proprietor families.

Deer Isle in the 1890s

The next one hundred years passed in relative peace and prosperity, and Deer Isle's residents discovered and exploited the natural abundance of the island and surrounding waters with typical Yankee industry. By the 1890s, Deer Isle's economy was highly diversified and prosperous. Deer Islers earned a living by fishing, shipping, granite quarrying, farming and serving a new and growing tourism business.

Deer Isle in the late nineteenth century was a socially vibrant and lively place. Its permanent population was over four thousand (considerably more than today's year-round population.) But like elsewhere in New England, comfort could only be earned through hard work, and it could also be suffused with sadness and loss. Many people lived to a ripe old age, but infant and child mortality was a problem on the island. For example, of the forty-two deaths recorded on the island in 1899, thirteen were people less than twenty-one years old, and six were less than two years of age.[8]

The northern and southern halves of the island were different places peopled by different types of characters. And Deer Isle remains so today. Bear in mind that Deer Isle (including Little Deer) is only twelve miles long and just over eight miles wide. On this small place, further reduced in area by numerous coves and harbors, two distinct cultures coexisted. In the north, where the original proprietor families settled, the land was kinder to farming. The south island is more rugged and difficult to farm—this is where most of the fishermen lived, and still do. The southern half of Deer Isle, including the small but accessible islands to the south, was where the granite quarries concentrated. The southern end of the island spawned a rough-and-tumble settlement called Green's Landing, which in 1897 seceded from the Town of Deer Isle to become Stonington.

Above: Salome Sellers, aged 106. Some Deer Islers lived to a very old age. Mrs. Sellers died at the age of 109 in 1909. *Courtesy of the Deer Isle–Stonington Historical Society.*

Opposite, top: Stonington Harbor in winter looking east. *Courtesy of the Deer Isle–Stonington Historical Society. From a collection by Dr. Benjamin Noyes.*

Opposite, bottom: Stonington Harbor in winter looking west. *Courtesy of the Deer Isle–Stonington Historical Society. From a collection by Dr. Benjamin Noyes.*

The icehouse on Stonington Harbor in the 1890s. Ice was and remains an essential on-board preservative for bait and certain catches. *Courtesy of the Deer Isle–Stonington Historical Society. From a collection by Dr. Benjamin Noyes.*

In the 1890s, Deer Isle was accessible only by boat. All inhabited islands off the Maine coast were connected to the mainland, and to each other, by boat. In the 1890s, Deer Isle was the scene of regular comings and goings on steamers, which ran regular schedules. In 1894, the Boston & Bangor Steamship Co. ran the steamer *Mount Desert* on a reliable daily schedule from Bar Harbor to Rockland via Green's Landing. In Rockland, passengers could either entrain or take another connecting steamer overnight to Boston. The Portland, Mt. Desert and Machias Steamboat Company took a more northerly route, running the *Frank Jones* on an all-day run from Rockland, north to Deer Isle on Eggemoggin Reach and ending up all the way downeast at Machiasport. Another steamer, the *City of Richmond*, ran from Bangor (also served by train) on the Penobscot River down to Deer Isle and back. A steamer ride from Stonington to Boston (connecting in Rockland) cost $3.00 in the summer and $2.25 in the winter. A ferry service ran regularly across the half-mile-wide Eggemoggin Reach, running from Sedgwick on the mainland to Scott's Landing on the island.

Deer Isle was active and populous enough to justify a local newspaper. Its first issue appeared for sale in March 1882 with the name *Deer Isle Gazette* on

Eggemoggin Landing, Little Deer Isle, in the late 1800s. Eggemoggin was a small enclave of homes created primarily by Philadelphians as an alternative to the more chic and established enclaves of Northeast, Bar and Winter Harbors. It was referred to as "Philly on the Rocks." *Courtesy of the Deer Isle–Stonington Historical Society.*

The steamer *J.T. Morse* at the north landing on Little Deer Isle. Prior to the Deer Isle-Sedgwick Bridge opening in 1939, steamers and ferries provided the only access to Deer Isle. Sedgwick is visible across Eggemoggin reach. *Courtesy of the Deer Isle–Stonington Historical Society.*

The Felsted Inn was one of several large hotels built on the western side of the island to accommodate the flood of rusticators who came to the Maine coast in the summers of the nineteenth century. The Felsted and others like it have burned or been torn down. *Courtesy of the Penobscot Marine Museum, Searsport, Maine.*

Captain Nelson Torrey and his daughters haying on Deer Isle in 1883. Like the Deer Isle sailors, Captain Torrey farmed or fished when not at sea. According to one New York reporter, all Maine sailors sailed yachts in the summer and farmed in the winter. Of course, farming in the Maine winter is impossible, and the Deer Islers found this opinion very amusing, but farming and fishing did fill the time and wallets when captain and crew were short of sea work. *Courtesy of the Deer Isle–Stonington Historical Society.*

its masthead. The island was beginning to develop its tourism businesses as well. Significant hotels were built to accommodate the influx of "rusticators." Planned communities, like the hamlet of Eggemoggin on Little Deer Isle, were established by groups of families interested in a summer getaway that was more affordable and less pretentious than Bar, Northeast and Winter Harbors.

The farmers in north Deer Isle worked the land hard. They had a bad habit of burning brush and stubble and then plowing the ashes back into the soil. This may have had a short-term benefit, but eventually, the soil was worked out. After the Civil War, many of the north Deer Isle farmers turned to the sea for their livelihoods. They fished multiple species. An 1898 report on the species landed in Hancock County, home to Deer Isle, showed that 34 percent of the dollar value of that year's catch was lobster. Other big-money catches were cod and other gill fish (26 percent), sardines (18 percent) and clams (10 percent). Today, lobster makes up nearly 80 percent of the cash value of landings in the state of Maine, the cod are essentially gone, clamming produces only 4 percent of revenues and the only new species added to the list since 1898 are eel, shrimp and worms at 2 percent each. The fishery in Maine today is dangerously undiversified.

By the 1890s, the transition from sail to steam in merchant and naval shipping was well underway. However, steam was adopted more slowly on coastal Maine—for two reasons. First, the fishermen of Maine had a significant investment in their sailing smacks, and apart from the heavy economic price of giving up vessels that had served them and their fathers well, traditions die hard in Maine. Second, for purposes other than regular schedules, such as ferry service or transporting perishable cargo, sail was still more cost effective than steam. Steamships required large amounts of coal to operate, and coal was scarce in Maine. In fact, most coal was delivered to Maine coaling stations by sail. In addition, small coal-fired steamers still had a relatively limited range due to the size of the bunkers required. For short hauls they were fine, but for long hauls larger vessels were required. The 1890s still saw the massive wooden "downeasters"—those magnificent four-, five- and sometimes six-masted schooners that carried bulk cargo like granite, lumber or ice south and brought back coal, iron, steel and other bulk material from the south and west.

In the 1890s Deer Islers were sailors, not steamer men. The lobstermen fished out of smacks like the famous Friendship sloop. Around twenty or twenty-five feet in length with a gaff-rigged main and cutter rig, these handy vessels could work a string of traps with one or two fishermen aboard. The wind in Maine is remarkably reliable—typically light in the

Opposite, top: The hermaphrodite brig *Venice* in Deer Island Thoroughfare off Stonington. The *Venice* was a late example of a Maine "downeaster"—heavy but reliable sailing vessels rigged for short-handed sailing that continued moving bulk freight such as granite and timber along the coast of Maine and New England into the twentieth century. *Courtesy of the Deer Isle–Stonington Historical Society. From a collection by Dr. Benjamin Noyes.*

Opposite, bottom: A fleet of lobster smacks departing Rockland Harbor. Located across Penobscot Bay from Deer Isle, Rockland was a major lobster fishing port in the 1890s. Rockland had railroad service and was often used by travelers to transfer from trains to steamers that provided scheduled service to Deer Isle and other islands along the coast of Maine. *Courtesy of the Penobscot Marine Museum, Searsport, Maine.*

Left: A young Maine fisherman underway. This young man is running an early engine-driven fishing boat, probably powered by a "make or break" single-cylinder gasoline engine. *Courtesy of the Penobscot Marine Museum, Searsport, Maine.*

morning and then freshening to ten to fifteen knots out of the southwest starting at about 11:30 or noon each summer day. The fishermen would ghost out to the fisheries at sunrise, haul the bulk of their traps in the relative calm water of the mid- to late morning and then pick up speed as the day progressed. (The same routine persists today, as one can hear the sound of diesel engines out of the Stonington and Deer Isle lobstering fleets rumbling across the water beginning at 4:30 a.m. every summer day but Sunday.) By the time the day's traps had all been hauled, the Deer Isle sailing fishermen of the 1890s had a freshening breeze to ride into the docks before unloading their catch at the canneries that dotted the coast. There the lobsters were immediately cooked, picked and the meat canned for shipment all over the country and around the world.

The hardy Maine schooner was a common sight along the coast in the 1890s. Fishing for cod and sardines, these rugged vessels trained many Deer Isle sailors in the art and science of handling a large fore-and-aft-rigged vessel in coastal waters. *Courtesy of the Penobscot Marine Museum, Searsport, Maine.*

Maine men fishing for sardines and alewife often worked from dories to haul nets and seines in the 1890s. A sailing smack is riding at anchor in the background. *Courtesy of the Penobscot Marine Museum, Searsport, Maine.*

The fishermen who worked the gill fisheries (cod, halibut and sardines) sailed their larger and highly efficient two-masted schooners farther offshore. Deer Isle fishermen, like their Gloucester counterparts to the south and west, worked the banks, shoals and offshore island waters in search of profitable concentrations of fish. Other schooners plied the coastal freight trade, moving bulk cargo from Maine port to Maine port and often making longer runs down to Boston, New York, Philadelphia and Baltimore. Masters at handling large fore-and-aft-rigged sailing vessels in coastal waters, these men were suited to sail the big cutters being built by the New York Yacht Club.

The challenge for the club was to find the best crew out of this bunch—the young, agreeable, reliable and self-disciplined types who could quickly form into a team of sailors capable of being away from home for as long as six months, living in the big city with all of its temptations and being under the intense spotlight of the world's most widely followed international sporting event. Finding great sailors on Deer Isle in the 1890s wasn't the problem; the problem was finding the thirty-five or forty sailors who could—and would—work together and work well under the odd circumstances of the highly publicized and elitist event called the America's Cup. To accomplish that took great men with great management skills, and in 1895, and to a lesser extent 1899, the New York Yacht Club had recruited several for their defense teams. They were motivated by publicity and pragmatism, as well as by the knowledge that the British would be putting a great boat in the water manned by their own homegrown team.

Wivenhoe: The Yacht Crew Nursery of England

Wivenhoe, in Essex, England, produced most of the skippers and crewmen that challenged for the cup in the late nineteenth century. Situated on the banks of the River Colne, the town stands seven miles north of the Thames estuary. Long before C. Oliver Iselin of New York recognized the wisdom of shipping a crew from a single seafaring town, the British had done so at Wivenhoe. The suffix "hoe" is translated from the old Anglo-Saxon as "ridge." It is speculated that "Wiven" may have derived from the family name of an important inhabitant of the place.

From the perspective of a sailor, Wivenhoe is geologically challenged in contrast with rocky Deer Isle. It has never been a deep-water port. The river is shallow and its mouth littered with sandbars. Despite its lack of natural gifts, Wivenhoe was home to a number of shipyards, the earliest dating back to that of the Quixleys in 1575. There were four "dokkes" on the river where freight and fish were unloaded.

By the end of the eighteenth century, Wivenhoe was well established as a center of fishing and coastal trade. Oysters came into dietary fashion, and Wivenhoe was recognized as a producer of the finest oysters in the area. The boatyards were busy building oyster smacks that the fishermen used to cultivate and harvest the beds downriver and in the Thames estuary. They also built ships. The subsidiary trades of rope, sail and barrel making also thrived at the time. As a clear indication that the maritime economy of Wivenhoe was maturing, in the late eighteenth century, citizens of Wivenhoe became investors in ships. They owned but didn't necessarily operate the vessels. In 1795, there were thirteen investors, and by 1805, there were twenty-eight.[9]

In the late 1700s, Wivenhoe's sail-racing culture began to take hold. The first recorded race for oyster smacks was held in 1783. They seemed to be fleet races pitting one town's best sailors against another's. This coincided with increasing leisure that follows prosperity and the early and general interest in sport in England at the time. But there were practical reasons for these races as well. Wivenhoe historian Nicholas Butler wrote:

> *Fishing smacks were not originally designed for speed, but eventually the need to get down river to where the shoal* [a large school of fish] *had been sighted before anyone else became of prime importance, and...there was sometimes a need to outsail the revenue cutters. Now the hard-won skills of the Colne fishermen were put to another use, for these races were the beginning of the local regattas and would very soon be turned to profit as well, in the service of the rich men who owned the big yachts.*[10]

The sailors of Wivenhoe were learning the value of speed under sail, and their skills were noticed by wealthy yachtsmen.

Like Deer Isle, Wivenhoe had developed a four-legged economy in the late nineteenth century, one of which was farming. Wivenhoe and the wider Colchester area produced agricultural produce for London and other urban centers that was then easily transported via the substantial Wivenhoe fleet to arrive fresh at the city markets. The second leg was fishing—the oldest and most sustained of the professions. Third was a form of quarrying. While on Deer Isle, particularly in Stonington, granite was the quarried export, watermen from Wivenhoe would sail out to the banks and dredge for a limestone called septaria, a component of concrete, and copperas, which is used in dyeing and ink making. The fourth was yachting. Unlike Deer Isle, which supplied the captains and crews, Wivenhoe supplied captains, crews, built the yachts and serviced them in winter storage as well. The town was a thriving and full-service maritime town.

Then, on April 22, 1884, the town was rocked by an earthquake. Wivenhoe was close to the epicenter of the quake and was the most heavily damaged village in England. Nicholas Butler wrote, "Wivenhoe looked as if it had been shelled."[11] Fortunately, there was only one casualty, but Wivenhoe suffered severe property damage and loss. These were days before ubiquitous insurance. A relief fund was set up, and almost £10,000 was raised, a sum roughly equivalent to £850,000 or $1.4 million in today's dollars. Wivenhoe rebuilt and went back to work—and to sailing.

The Wivenhoe yachting culture was nearly identical to what the Deer Islers were beginning to experience at the same time. Butler is worth quoting again:

Life was always hard for these self-employed men, the toughest, hardiest members of the community, yet they were their own masters and some declined to surrender their independence to crewing in the summer. Nevertheless, the competition for places aboard the big yachts was fierce. Crewing had several advantages. First of all, there was a regular wage, which in a racing yacht might be doubled or even trebled by prize money.

The crewmen had two important perquisites: he was clothed and fed. Every season, each man was kitted out by the owner. His uniform would last the rest of the year and used or unwanted items be passed down the family or given away. When a fisherman left home, he took most of his larder with him. The wife whose husband crewed, and was therefore away for the season, could expect to feed their family properly.

Life aboard a cruising yacht was, of course, much easier, as, except for the captain and engineer, the crewman was more of a domestic servant than an athlete. Like a good servant, he was blind to things it was not his business to know. One crewman recalled an owner who was a stockbroker. His wife and children were given a fortnight's holiday aboard his yacht, but at other times he was joined by his mistress, nominally his secretary. The crew, reared on a totally different moral code, had to accept this in silence. Another crewman recalled that a young lady, the daughter of a rich and important man, thought nothing of bathing in the nude. The crew might be present, but since they were only crew, the lady was alone.[12]

Butler goes on to discuss less titillating matters:

> *Crewing had its mystique: the thrills of competing in a prestigious sport, of adding to the town's considerable reputation, of escaping from the Colne estuary, seeing different places and people, and returning with souvenirs and stories.*[13]

Much the same can be said about the Deer Isle men who were paid to travel to New York to sail against the Wivenhovians in the America's Cup races of 1895 and 1899.

Wivenhoe captains were very well paid. They earned about five pounds per week plus a two-pound-per-week retainer through the winter. In 1890, this was equivalent to twenty-five dollars per week in the United States, comparable to what an American yacht captain could expect to earn. The captains were also employers to be respected. Butler wrote:

> *Because the captain chose his men and because of his unquestionable skill and experience, he had considerable authority over them. The crew might include younger relations, but the captain was "Sir." The captains retained their Essex burrs but might be on first-name terms with their employers. These men had triumphed in a harsh world and were accorded a tremendous prestige.*[14]

Wivenhoe produced generations of successful officers and crew for Britain's yachts. American skippers and owners occasionally competed against these sailors when after 1851 they again visited England for the racing season. Charlie Barr himself sailed *Vigilant* across the Atlantic in 1893 after the America's Cup race against Lord Dunraven's first challenger, *Valkyrie II* (which was sunk in a collision in 1894). Barr raced against Wivenhovians and knew they could sail well. He brought that knowledge back to New York and to C. Oliver Iselin upon his record-setting transatlantic return in 1894. Barr, Iselin and Haff all knew that if they could find an American town or area similar to Wivenhoe—a place where the sailing culture was deep, the crewmen all knew and respected each other and the work ethic was strong— then perhaps they could assemble an all-American crew to match the best of Wivenhoe. Deer Isle turned out to be just that place.

Chapter 3

NEW YORKERS COME TO DEER ISLE

Captain Haff went to Deer Isle, Maine, where with the help of a local mariner,
he hand-picked a salty group of American Vikings.[15]

Why did the New York Yacht Club send emissaries all the way to Deer Isle, Maine, to recruit a yacht racing crew? The epicenters of yachting on the East Coast were Long Island Sound and, to a lesser extent, coastal New Jersey. Hank Haff, the accomplished America's Cup veteran and skipper of the new Herreshoff boat, *Defender*, was himself a product of Long Island and its sailing culture. The region was loaded with good sailors. This chapter will address the above, and the further ones will examine why the New Yorkers came back to Deer Isle when it came time to man *Columbia*.

EARLY CONNECTIONS: DEER ISLE, YACHTING AND THE AMERICA'S CUP

The connection between Deer Isle and the America's Cup itself extends back to at least 1886, when Haff was an established name in elite yacht-racing circles, including the America's Cup. It was then that Haff, a member of the defense boat *Mayflower*, first worked with George Conant of Deer Isle. Conant was second mate of *Mayflower*, having already established his own reputation as a competent officer aboard yachts. *Mayflower* defeated *Galatea* in two September races—the first by over twelve minutes and the second by nearly half an hour. It was clearly a faster boat than the well appointed and heavy *Galatea*, a yacht outfitted more for luxury than speed. The American officers aboard, including Conant, directed a professional crew of Scandinavians as was common in racing circles of the day.

In 1887, Conant again officered an America's Cup boat aboard *Volunteer* as second mate. Haff wasn't the skipper, but C. Oliver Iselin was in the crew. Iselin would later organize the *Defender* and *Columbia* defenses (as well as others) and, over the course of training and racing, would come to know Conant well. Long before the New York Yacht Club came to Deer Isle in 1895, the characteristics of the Deer Isle sailor were well known. Iselin and Haff both had firsthand experience with these men through George Conant and others.

Hank Haff grew up on Long Island. In 1895, he lived in Islip, a middle-class community on Long Island's southern coast. Like many professional yacht captains in the Victorian era, Haff started out fishing. John Rousmaniere said the following at Haff's America's Cup Hall of Fame induction in 2004:

> *Like almost all racing skippers before the twentieth century, Hank Haff started out as a professional fisherman. When he first sailed, it was in catboats that worked the waters off the south shore of Long Island, New York. Like many fishermen, he did a little yachting during the summer. His abilities as a racing sailor and crew boss were quickly recognized, and he rose to the position of "advisor" (what we call tactician) in two America's Cup winners: Mischief in 1881 and Mayflower in 1886.*

Haff was not an elitist. His waterman origins ensured that he understood and respected the crew. There is ample evidence in the historical record that Hank Haff was well liked by his crewmen.

In June 1899, a reporter from the *Sun* (New York) interviewed George Conant. Conant told the reporter his side of the story of how the New York Yacht Club first came to Deer Isle:

> *"It came about like this," said Capt. George. "Thirteen years ago when I was second mate of the Mayflower, when we licked the Galatea, Capt. Hank Haff he said, 'This beatin' the British is all right, George, but I ain't satisfied.' Says he, 'Here these races are for the America's Cup. They're sailed in American boats, built of American material*

The great Henry "Hank" Haff aboard a yacht in the 1890s. His trademark beard indicates a good breeze over the port side. *Image © Mystic Seaport, Rosenfeld Collection, #Y1171. Photographer: Charles Edwin Bolles.*

> *by American working men and sailed by American masters,* [and] *by thunderation they ought to be manned by an American crew! George, is there any reason why we couldn't have an all-American crew? Couldn't we get a full crew of Deer Islers?' And I says, 'We could, Capt. Hank,'* [and] *he says, 'Let's do it.'"* It was 1893 that Capt. Hank Haff had his way, and when he came to select the crew for his next cup defender, he sent to Deer Isle, and out of the 900 sailormen available and anxious to go on the yacht, the 33 necessary ones were chosen. Conant, the second mate, shipped most of the crew.[16]

While a well-respected sailor and officer aboard America's Cup boats, George Conant's accuracy as an historian is less clear. Conant was involved, but he was one of several important individuals who connected the Club with the Island.

Charles Oliver Iselin ("Ollie" to his closest friends) was equally important. Born in 1854 in New York City, Iselin was the grandson of a Swiss-born emigrant. His father, Adrian Iselin, was a successful businessman as well and was a significant financial supporter of both the *Defender* and *Columbia* defenses. C. Oliver was a success in his own right, initially as a banker, and later among the most capable organizers of America's Cup campaigns in the long history of the event. He also married well. After his first wife, Fannie Garner, had died, he married Edith Hope Goddard, a Providence, Rhode Island heiress in 1894. C. Oliver and Hope (she dropped Edith after their marriage) made a formidable pair in the high stakes yachting culture of New York City and Long Island Sound, as well as the refined society circles of Aiken, South Carolina, where they maintained their winter home that Hope named "Hopelands."

The couple's summer home was a Georgian brick waterfront mansion in New Rochelle, New York. They called it "All View." The mansion is sited on Premium Point, commanding an unobstructed southerly view of Long Island Sound and all of its yachting and shipping traffic. There is evidence that Iselin occasionally visited Bar Harbor, Maine, just fifteen miles east of Deer Isle. While there, he stayed with acquaintances from the New York Yacht Club in that fashionable enclave. Many of the Bar Harbor yachts were manned by Deer Isle men, and it is likely that Iselin met more than a few on these visits. He may have met Captain Fred Weed, who he later retained to recruit the *Defender* crew on Deer Isle while visiting Northeast Harbor, the equally tony town a few miles south of Bar Harbor. Fred Weed resided in Northeast Harbor, having removed there from Deer Isle in the late 1880s.

The Iselins had three children: Fannie, Nora and Oliver. Evidence suggests that the Iselins were a devoted couple and C. Oliver a good father. For example, he gave his son an allowance, although not an excessive one. Young Oliver received ten dollars as a birthday gift from his father on August 23, 1899, in the midst of the *Columbia* campaign.

C. Oliver Iselin was the consummate general manager. While intensely involved with the details of yacht-racing rules, design, construction, management and campaigning, he was also extraordinarily skilled at choosing the right people for the job and then encouraging them to do their jobs well. He was also capable of setting his silver spoon aside and working hard to accomplish what he needed to. For example, although high-born and a successful banker in his mid-forties, Iselin was willing to serve as an ordinary crewman aboard *Volunteer* in 1887 as it defeated G.L. Watson's *Thistle*. Aboard *Volunteer*, he witnessed firsthand Hank Haff's competence in helming a big cutter. When Iselin later rose to syndicate chief for the 1895 series, he hired Haff to skipper *Defender* based on his experience under Haff as a crewman and direct observer of Haff's capabilities in sail competition.

Iselin surrounded himself with good people, and those chosen for his inner circle tended to stay. He and Hope were married for nearly forty years until his death in 1932 (Hope died in 1970 at the age of 102). His close friends from the New York Yacht Club Woodbury Kane and Herbert C. Leeds served with him in the afterguards of five campaigns: *Vigilant* (1893), *Defender* (1895), *Columbia* (1899), *Columbia* again (1901) and *Reliance* (1903). Hank Haff sailed for Iselin in *Vigilant* and *Defender*. Cornelius Vanderbilt and J.P. Morgan, two excessively demanding people, entrusted Iselin with the reputations of the cup, the club and, to some extent, themselves, as they repeatedly supported him in his role as syndicate manager over eleven years and five successful America's Cup defenses.

C. Oliver Iselin, skilled manager and fierce competitor, saw the wisdom of an all-American crew. The concept had both publicity value as well as practical advantages. The America's Cup races were hugely popular. In the 1890s, the nation's newspapers were filled with stories both speculative and factual about the America's Cup. Patriotism was running high and would reach a fever pitch when the explosion that sank the battleship *Maine* in Havana Harbor triggered the Spanish-American War in 1898. An all-American (and somewhat ironically all-Maine) crew was an effective answer to frequent criticism—particularly in the English press—of the Scandinavian "mercenaries" who handled the American boats as they sailed against England's native Wivenhovians. The concept played well to American nationalistic sentiments and laid to rest the British criticism.

Not everyone thought that Iselin's new approach to crew recruiting was a good one. It was controversial and provoked an active debate, both before and after the races. On the one hand, writers like America's Cup historian (and rival to Iselin) Thomas Lawson were largely supportive. He wrote:

> *Defender was commanded by Capt. "Hank" Haff and manned by an entire crew of Yankee sailors shipped at Deer Isle, Maine, a nursery of yacht sailors now as famous as ever was Wivenhoe in England. They were the first wholly American crew employed on a cup defender, as all former crews contained numbers of Swedes and Norwegians, who for many years were relied upon as our best yachting sailors. The Deer Isle men were superior to Scandinavians in racing work chiefly because of their higher order of intelligence.* [17]

C. Oliver Iselin's steam launch approaching *Defender* in 1895 carrying members of the afterguard. *From bow to stern*: C. Oliver Iselin, Herbert C. Leeds and Woodbury Kane. These three men were involved with five America's Cup defenses from 1893 to 1903. The launchman is Harry O'Dell. *Image © Mystic Seaport, #1951.15.25.*

C. Oliver Iselin's steam launch arriving at *Defender*'s starboard side. Iselin is leaning toward *Defender* helping to fend off from the new yacht's gleaming white topsides. Haff stands on deck immediately above, and Herreshoff is observing from astern. *Defender* sailed through its trial races painted white, but when she raced *Valkyrie III*, Iselin had her painted light blue. *Image © Mystic Seaport, #1951.15.10.*

Rockland Harbor in the early 1900s. The Maine schooner and its "American Vikings" still dominated the fishing and bulk shipping trades. *Courtesy of the Penobscot Marine Museum, Searsport, Maine.*

However, early in the following century, Nathanael Herreshoff's son, L. Francis Herreshoff, a wonderful writer and himself a noted designer and sailor of highly successful racing and cruising boats, took a very different posture:

> *While no doubt Maine fishermen are picturesque characters and good on smacks with a crew of one or two, they were not to be compared with the crews of various nationalities which had specialized in large yacht racing.*[18]

It is somewhat ironic that Lawson, Iselin's rival and sometimes critic, would come to admire the Deer Isle men, while L. Francis Herreshoff would not. After all, the Deer Isle crews sailed his father's racers to victory. Perhaps, as we shall see, the Deer Isle men's frictions with their commanding officers in 1899 colored Herreshoff's long-term view of these "American Vikings."

Hank Haff Visits Deer Isle

When Hank Haff visited Deer Isle in March 1895, he was joining in on an already established cycle of work. Yacht skippers or their agents had begun visiting the island in the winter and early spring each year to hire hands for the upcoming yachting season. This is how men like George Conant had originally entered the business. It was a form of migratory labor. Recruiters would come to the island looking for new hires, and those Deer Islers who had worked in yachts before were often asked who the best new recruits might be.

Having convinced the New York Yacht Club syndicate that an all-American crew made good publicity and racing sense, Iselin called on Hank Haff to make a trip downeast. It's not known whether Iselin or Haff chose Deer Isle as the destination. Both were so deeply involved with big-yacht sailing and racing that it probably was a joint decision. Deer Isle was home to a large concentration of good sailors, so why go anywhere else? Haff departed New York in early March by train bound for Boston. He arrived at South Station and probably spent the night in the city. It is probable that he stayed at the Mariner's House in the North End or a boardinghouse similar to it. The Mariner's House is situated midway between South and North Stations on North Square, near the delights of Hanover Street and the working waterfront of Boston's inner harbor, and was well known to Deer Isle men who sailed coasters to Boston loaded with lumber or granite. Still in operation today, Boston's Mariner's House has been the temporary home of sailors arriving in Boston by train and by sea since 1847. The Mariner's House would have offered Haff clean accommodations and meals for a reasonable price. The following morning, Haff boarded the train for downeast Maine. In the 1890s, profitable and reliable train service ran from Boston all the way east to Ellsworth and beyond, carrying freight, local passengers and summer folk to the steamers or carriage services that then brought them to and from their cottages on Vinalhaven Island, Islesboro Island, North Deer Isle, Deer Isle, Bar Harbor, Northeast Harbor, Hancock Point and Winter Harbor on Schoodic Point. Haff booked for Rockland, probably arriving late in the afternoon. He spent another night ashore in Rockland (a boomtown in the 1890s) at one of the many hotels or boardinghouses that lined the busy waterfront. The fishing and granite businesses were in full swing. Hundreds of coastal schooners, bankers and fishing smacks worked out of Rockland on the western shore of Penobscot Bay. One reason that the town was so

The Ark, still operating today as the Pilgrim's Inn, in the heart of Deer Isle village. The Ark is where Hank Haff, Captain Fred Weed and George Conant met with candidates for the *Defender* America's Cup crew in the winter of 1895. *Courtesy of the Penobscot Marine Museum, Searsport, Maine.*

prosperous was that its topography allowed train tracks to be brought close to shore, easing the transfer of bulk cargo from train to ship or ship to train.

The following morning, Haff would have caught the steamer *J.T. Morse*, which ran regular service from the northern end of Deer Isle on its way to and from Bar Harbor, or the *Mount Desert*, which competed with the *J.T. Morse* by taking the more southerly route and landing at Green's Landing (later Stonington) on the southern end of the island. He would have arrived at the landing and been met by one of the many Deer Islers who had sailed under his command in seasons gone by—perhaps George Conant. He would then have been transported to the Ark boardinghouse in Deer Isle village. Now called the Pilgrim's Inn, the Ark was built in 1793 and was the site of important town meetings and events like the *Defender* crew recruitment interviews.

Haff had very likely telegraphed Conant in advance, advising him of his intentions and arrival date. The message Haff sent did not survive, but it must have said that he would be interested in meeting with a well-respected, well-connected and retired captain who could help him find the best sailing team Deer Isle could assemble on short notice. Conant (and probably others) recommended Captain Fred P. Weed.

In a notebook entry dated 1899 authored by J.N. Taylor and held at the Deer Isle–Stonington Historical Society, Fred Weed was described as follows:

And no man in America is better qualified to distinguish between good and poor capabilities in a seaman. When Capt. Weed was 8 years old, he was cook on the little schooner Franklin of Frankfort at $3 per month, and up to age 14 he was employed on coasters and on 50 and 100-ton boats running to the banks for fish. From 14 to 17, he was on the brig New World, the ship Charles and Jane, and the bark Fleet Eagle, engaged in the West India trade. At the age of 17, he shipped as second mate of the bark R.H. Knight, was mate of her one year later and her captain at 20. From this time on, Capt. Weed's career was remarkable. He was for 29 years master of vessels, and during that period he rounded Cape Horn four times and made port in Russia, Norway, Germany, France, England, Ireland, Spain, Italy, Turkey, Greece, Asia, Africa, Japan, China, Brazil, Chile, Peru, Hawaii and Mexico. He is one of the very few men in New England armed with a certificate which licenses him to take any kind of vessels to any place in the world.

In September 1895, *Outing* magazine published an article by R.B. Burchard titled "The Cup Champions and Their Crews." It is worth quoting at length. Although written in the florid and romantic style popular in the late nineteenth century, it touches on a number of the important themes of the Deer Isle crews' story, telling of the "bold and original" strategy of going to Deer Isle to recruit a ready-made crew of excellent sailors:

The officers and men of the Defender are the heart and soul in the contest. The crew have already become famous from the sentiment through which they were chosen, rather than because of anything they have yet accomplished. The selection of the crew of the Defender was a bold and original departure from custom. It was probably instigated by practical motives, but, from the circumstances of the case, it could not fail to excite a patriotic sentiment. In the absence of any neighboring villages of trained yachtsmen who live in clans, as they do in England, it has hitherto been necessary to pick up a miscellaneous crew, generally of Scandinavians. These men are glad during the summer to exchange the hard life on the traders and the steam liners for the better living and lighter work on the yachts. Some of them make excellent crews, but they scatter over the globe in the winter and can with difficulty be kept together from year to year. Even if they had equal alertness with the American and the English sailors, they would be at a disadvantage through ignorance of the language. There is no denying that the Swedes are splendid sailors; they climb like cats, swim like seals and work like beavers. The disadvantage, however, in the employment of mixed foreign crews is obvious, and the wonder is that no one has thought of Mr. Iselin's excellent scheme before. Down on the coast of Maine are a race of American sailors. These men have been sailing boats all their lives, just as the best English racing crews have done, as fishermen.

The fisherman's life is continued racing. It's get out with your seines, make your haul and scurry to port before the increased supply has lowered the price of the catch. Never was keener racing than that between the fishermen of Wivenhoe, on the Clyde, or our own Gloucester. And so, Mr. Iselin sent Captain Haff down among the "thorofares" of the Maine Islands to cast about to see what he could secure in the way of a brand new American crew. The Captain found what he wanted and did not have to go far from Rockland to get it. He went to one place, Deer Island [sic]. Like all the islands of the main group, it has raised a stock of men such as heroes are made of when opportunity offers.

Haff took up residence at the Ark and called for volunteers. He was offering an opportunity for a long summer of work, but the work he offered was more interesting, easier and paid better than anything the Deer Isle sailors could expect at home. Many Deer Islers had been to New York before as sailors or officers aboard the island's coastal freighters, but some of the younger men had not, and they looked forward to getting away from the island for a trip to the city. Haff's package proved to be irresistible. Estimates are that about three hundred men responded to Haff's proposition. Haff and Weed took the applications and, as Burchard wrote, deliberately chose a crew that was composed of reliable men who could be counted on to coalesce into an effective crew for the big metal cutter then under construction at the Herreshoff yard in Bristol, Rhode Island:

It was town-meeting day, and he said to the people, "I want men from among you to sail the new cup defender!" Well! He owned the place. He set up his headquarters in a venerable mansion, a hundred and six years old, and now the leading boarding house on the island. Here, before a blazing log fire, the famous skipper of the Great South Bay, supported on either hand by two of the magnates of the place, Captain Weed and Captain Conant, received the aspirants to fame and sport who lined up before him— the best blood of Deer Island [sic]—always ready for sport or struggle on the deep. The successful candidates were selected, with the advice of the local fathers, after much secret deliberation, and the result was announced.

When Haff, Conant and Weed were done with interviews and deliberations, they offered thirty-five men the job. All accepted. Generally, the crewmen selected had several common characteristics. All had lifelong sailing experience and were well-respected watermen. In 1899, J.N. Taylor would write about the specific sailing experience sought by Iselin and Weed in selecting both the 1895 and 1899 Deer Isle crews:

A leap at conclusions might lead parson to think that among deep-sea sailors would be found the right kind of material for a racing yacht's crew. Quite the contrary, however, is nearer to being correct. Racing yachts, says Capt. Weed, require a different class of men than those employed on seagoing vessels. Everything is different, and to get an able crew, it is necessary to pick men who have been schooled in craft as closely resembling the racers as possible. The first requirement is, of course, to get men who have had experience, and experience secured on vessels ranging in measurement from 10 to 100 tons is much better than that secured on larger boats. The next requirements are pluck, agility, presence of mind and sobriety. Drinking men are not to be depended upon, and a man with liquor in his skin aboard ship is handicapped in thought and movement, even if he has not enough aboard to telegraph his condition to the onlookers.

The issue of sobriety was paramount. Weed, Haff, Iselin and the New York Yacht Club looked for men who could stay sober throughout the summer despite the proximity of New York City. A *Sun* reporter wrote:

The average Deer Isle man is not egotistic, and he'll assert that the world has a mistaken idea about the isle's growing the best sailormen in the world. He'll tell you that the sailormen up there are just average, but then he'll go on to say: 'Ye see the boys from here don't drink. Of course now and then you'll find one that does, but if you scratch him, you'll find he ain't a real Deer Isle man. Maybe he was born here but his ancestors don't go back fur.

Many came from the same families. The *Defender* crew shipped two Barbours, both as quartermasters, although Bently Barbour developed an illness (reported as appendicitis) that landed him in a Newport, Rhode Island hospital during the trials. He later died in May 1896 at the age of twenty-five. There were two each from the Staples, Robbins, Stinson and Scott families; three Brays; and five Haskells. These were a mix of brothers and cousins, and most had worked together before in various capacities and command arrangements. Bill Haviland, anthropologist and lifelong resident of the island, has remarked that one of the attributes of the Deer Isle America's Cup crews that impressed him the most was their ability to leave behind previous command relationships and assume the new ones imposed by Captain Haff and his sailing master, Norman Terry, and first mate, James Berry, neither of whom had met the Deer Islers until they arrived in Bristol, Rhode Island, later that spring. Among the Deer Islers were a number of young men who had served as officers on yachts or merchant vessels but had asked to serve as ordinary seamen aboard *Defender*. Their flexibility enabled them to take Haff up on his offer of easier work at better pay, and, perhaps for a handful, the prospect of representing the New York Yacht Club in their races against the British added to the appeal. They did what they had to do, and they did it well.

Burchard embellishes the culmination of the recruiting visit by quoting a reporter from the *New York Herald* (who was not present) who attributed the following speech to Haff:

> *Captain Haff is recorded as saying: "I have been told that some of you have been mates and even masters of vessels, but you will not be either during the service for which I have come to Deer Island* [sic] *to ship you. You will be in the forecastle, and the work on the yacht will be hard, and there will be plenty of it, night as well as day sometimes. There has been a great deal said about an American crew, if they were got to ether, not wanting to obey orders, of jealousies arising and that all hands in a short time would want to be captain. If there are any of you here who have the faintest suspicion that they will feel so in the future, I don't care to go further with such, but if you come with me and you help, as you know how, to keep the old cup, you'll never regret it. You will be treated like men, and next fall, if we are successful, we'll have some fun."*

The same reporter, still *in absentia*, was quoted by Burchard as saying that Fred Weed, the island's "Nestor" (the sage advisor to younger sailors) said:

I have known every one of you since you were children and have followed you in your various ventures at sea. All of you have good reputations, and it is my wish and that of your fellow townsmen that you maintain them. We think that Captain Haff has honored Deer Island [sic] in coming here for his crew for the cup defender, and you should feel that it is an honor for you to help keep that old prize. Every true American values it. The wealthy gentlemen who are building the yacht that is likely to defend it are true patriots—they have that kind of patriotism we like and prize up here in Maine, where every man is a sailor and knows what the old flag means. Now, I will follow you boys this summer very closely. So will every other Deer Islander. If any of you should prove unworthy of your place and are discharged for bad conduct, we don't want to see you again. But we know that you will be men, that you will obey orders cheerfully and willingly, and work for the cause. Do this, and we'll welcome you heartily upon your return.

While it is highly unlikely that Captains Haff and Weed, educated by life experiences, worldwide travel and hard work, actually said these words, it is clear that the editors of the *Herald* wished to emphasize the publicity value of an all-American and, of course, highly patriotic crew. The quotes do raise one important point. The men selected by Haff and Weed did care about their reputations, both while in New York sailing for the "wealthy gentlemen" and, more importantly, upon their return to their island town. Island communities have subtle but powerful governance mechanisms. People tend to cooperate, avoiding overt conflict whenever possible. It is difficult to get away from each other on a ship or on an island, and Haff and Weed knew this. Furthermore, by recruiting multiple members of the "best" island families—families that had already established themselves as respected members of the community—they further reinforced this fact. The crews from Deer Isle already constituted an effective and collaborative team and, at least in the context of their relationships with each other, had compelling reasons to remain that way. However, as shall be seen through their frictions with Charlie Barr four years later, when confronted by a common enemy, they were equally capable of deciding *en masse* that their services were better employed elsewhere.

Those who had experience aboard yachts or coastal fore-and-aft-rigged vessels were usually assigned the more important jobs like quartermaster or masthead man. The youngest, "Coo" Eaton, was twenty years old, and the oldest, "Harsee" Davis, was fifty. Most were in their twenties or early thirties. About two-thirds of them had wives and families. Most importantly, primarily through the insights of Fred Weed, the successful candidates were known on the island as solid citizens and reliable workers. Their names and positions are shown in Appendix II.

The *Sun* reporter managed to identify an essential difference between a Deer Isle man and someone who was not a member of a well-established island family, and that difference persists even today. With only two exceptions (Elmer Hamblen and Charles Porter), all of the *Defender* crewmen were either descended from Hosmer's "proprietor" families (those families who resided on the island prior to January 1, 1784, and therefore qualified for the initial one-hundred-acre allocation of land upon the town's incorporation in 1789) or from immigrants who had arrived from the mainland before 1800. Bentley and Irvin Barbour were descended from Solomon Barbour, who arrived on the island in 1793. Coo Eaton was descended from William Eaton, who came to the island in 1762 and was a proprietor. William E. Hardy's ancestor was Peter Hardy, also a proprietor and immigrant to the island in 1775. John E. Billings's ancestor John Billings arrived in 1763. The *Defender* and the later *Columbia* crews were composed of Deer Isles' finest sailors but also tended to include members of the ancient families of the island.

COMPENSATION

By March 1895, Haff was writing confident letters to Iselin. On March 16, he wrote:

> *About the men. I could get some men for $35 per mo. & $5.00 extra if they stayed the season, but not the best. I have promised to give them $35.00 per mo. & $10.00 extra per mo. if they give satisfaction & stay the season & $4.00 for every race won. They understand that if they want to leave or are discharged for any reason they are to be paid off with $35.00 per mo., the $10.00 extra & race money to be paid at the end of the season & we are to pay their passage to the boat. I had them sign no paper but they will sign any contract you may wish them to. Every man is strongly recommended by one that I have confidence in & they talked as though they would take a lively interest in the matter & I believe they will.*

What Haff was offering, and what Iselin ultimately agreed to pay the Deer Isle men, was substantially richer than what they received as working merchantmen or fishermen. Haff's visit to Deer Isle followed closely on the heels of the Panic of 1893, America's great economic downturn of the nineteenth century. As is the case today, Maine was the first to feel the effects of economic recession—and among the last to recover from it. It is likely that the Deer Islers had suffered from a diminution in shipping trade and a reduced appetite for their farming and fishery products. Demand for the island's granite and tourist hospitality had also fallen off. What Haff was offering seemed very attractive compared to what they had recently endured or could reasonably expect in the near future.

According to government records, in the 1890s, an experienced seaman in the U.S. merchant marine earned on average $25.00 per month, of course without the prospect of race money or retention bonus. A first mate earned $35.00 per month and a captain $125.00 each month. Haff was offering a sailor 80 percent more than the average merchantman if he stayed on the *Defender* team the entire season plus an additional 16 percent over a merchantman's wages in race bonus. The local Deer Isle newspaper, the *Weekly Gazette*, reported that lobsters were fetching $0.08 each at the dock in the 1880s. Fisheries records from the same era show that a good lobsterman might land $50.00 of lobsters in a month, but that was a gross take. Out of that $50.00, he had to pay for the expense of the boat (including fuel if it was powered) plus the cost of his fishing gear, so he might have netted $25.00 per month in exchange for very hard work.

Officers (George Conant as second officer was the only Deer Isle man so ranked) were paid $50.00 per month on *Defender* plus a $10.00 monthly retention bonus if they remained the entire season. Quartermasters (of which there were four) were paid $40.00 plus $10.00 retention if they stayed. Officers and quartermasters were paid $5.00 and $4.00 in victory bonus for each race won. *Defender* won three races, so a Deer Isle crewman who worked mid-June through mid-September would have earned up to $147.00 in wages and bonuses for the season. As an ordinary merchant seaman or lobsterman, he would have earned $75.00, or perhaps $105.00 if he'd shipped out aboard a coaster as a mate. On the basis of money alone, Haff's offer would have been difficult for an intelligent man to reject. It is no surprise that hundreds turned out for recruiting interviews at the Ark.

To assess whether Iselin thought the Deer Isle men were cost-effective, it is possible to compare their compensation not only with merchant mariners or lobstermen but also with other monthly employees familiar to the syndicate members. For example, the Mystic Seaport Museum's Iselin Papers Collection shows that in 1899, C. Oliver Iselin paid his household staff as follows:

INDIVIDUAL	POSITION	MONTHLY WAGE
L.A. Hampton	Private Secretary	$125.00
Antoine Besse	Chef	$80.00
Herbert Lawyer	Butler	$60.00
Harry Odell	Launchman	$60.00
Poppley	Coachman	$60.00
George Gjoerloff	Valet	$50.00
John Almsted	Second Man	$40.00
Louise	Maid	$20.00

A Deer Isle sailor was paid roughly the same as a valet or "second man" in Iselin's New Rochelle household staff. L.A. Hampton, Iselin's private secretary, was paid as much as a sea captain. The income differentials between New York and Deer Isle for comparable jobs were as wide then as they are now.

Haff also agreed to pay for the sailors' transportation to and from Bristol or New York. The Deer Isle men incurred those expenses themselves and were reimbursed by Fred Weed later in the season. During the *Columbia* campaign (the *Defender* accounts are not preserved), island recruiter Fred Weed was paid $3,488.58 on August 12, 1899, presumably for travel and other expenses reimbursement for the Deer Isle crewmen who had made the trip. In April 1899, Iselin paid Weed $50.00 plus a pewter tankard for his recruiting services.

In addition to travel expenses, the Deer Isle men were provided a white duck racing uniform, sailor's cap and rubber-soled shoes. The shoes cost the syndicate eighty cents a pair and were purchased from the National Rubber Company. The crew was also allowed seventy cents per day for their mess, which was typically served aboard *Defender's* tender the *Hattie Palmer*.

A receipt in the New York Yacht Club archives in Hank Haff's writing notes:

Received from C. Oliver Iselin, Esq. the sum of four thousand two hundred thirty 48/100 dollars for wages & prize money of crew from September 1st to September 15th, 1895.

—*H.C. Haff*

Like most merchant vessels and yachts at the time, the crew was "paid off" at the end of a voyage or contracted work period. And like any merchantman in the 1890s, the captain or his designated officer was responsible for distributing wages and bonuses to the subordinate officers and crew. There was no income tax, Social Security, Medicare, workers' compensation premiums or other payroll withholdings in the 1890s, so Iselin gave Haff a sum of money, and Haff distributed it in accordance with his agreements with the men. The men then went home, humble heroes returning to their small island town with cash in their pockets and pride in their hearts.

Chapter 4

DEFENDER, 1895

Victory and International Controversy

When Captain Haff, his officers and his crew of Deer Isle men arrived in Bristol, Rhode Island, in early June 1895 to take up the mantle as defenders of the America's Cup, they did not know that they were to become actors in a drama that would nearly destroy the reputations of great men, their yacht clubs and of the America's Cup itself.

The *Defender-Valkyrie III* series on the water was brief and brutal. As one commentator put it in September 1895, the three races were a "fluke, a foul and a fizzle." The series is best remembered for the off-water controversies initiated by challenger Lord Dunraven, who had returned for his second run at the cup.

There were three disputes, and the two that mattered most would directly involve the men from Deer Isle. The one that mattered least was the continued uncontrollable spectator fleet that carried paying passengers out to the racecourse. Lord Dunraven had complained about this in the 1893 races, and he continued to press for better control or even a change in race venue to somewhere other than New York (he suggested Marblehead). His request was denied, and his complaints were heard and acknowledged but not very effectively acted upon.

The second dispute was "The Foul," a split-second event captured by Russ Kramer in his marvelous painting and, unfortunately for the challenger, by photographers aboard observation vessels. During tight pre-start maneuvers for the second race, maneuvers complicated by the unruly spectator fleet, *Valkyrie III* and *Defender* collided. The collision damaged *Defender*'s rigging and placed extraordinary demands on its crew. The Deer Isle men made on-the-fly temporary repairs under difficult conditions. Their work enabled *Defender* to complete the race, although under protest. It lost the race on the course, but to Lord Dunraven's disgust was awarded the win later that day in the Race Protest Committee meeting.

The third dispute was the most destructive of all, as it ruined whatever good sporting reputation remained for Dunraven, threatened the honor of America's wealthiest and most influential and ambitious yachtsmen, led certain pundits to conclude that the America's Cup event was dead and embroiled the Deer Isle crewmen in the affair for the remainder of the year.

Lord Dunraven privately and then upon his return to the UK publicly accused Iselin of illegally adding ballast to *Defender*, thereby lowering it in the water and extending its waterline length. Absent a rating adjustment, under certain sailing conditions, a longer waterline would have given *Defender* an unlawful advantage over *Valkyrie III*. Iselin and the New York Yacht Club responded with surprise and indignation and then arranged a detailed inquiry and investigation to clear their names. Dunraven returned from Britain to testify, and an emissary was sent to Deer Isle to recall a number of crewmen back to New York, as well as to secure written affidavits to counter Dunraven's claims. In the end, Iselin was vindicated, and a Dunraven offer to resign his honorary membership to the New York Yacht Club was accepted. Dunraven never raced yachts in international competition again.

New evidence uncovered during research for this book—evidence sourced directly from a Deer Isle crewman—suggests that an attitude existed on the American side in 1899 that if also present and acted upon in 1895 would have meant that Dunraven was correct. In an interview with the last surviving Deer Isle America's Cup crewman, a sailor aboard *Columbia*, he revealed how the Iselin boats were ballasted and the fact that those methods were kept secret, adding fresh fuel to this smoldering Dunraven fire.

DESIGNING THE NEW *DEFENDER*

Edward Burgess, designer of three America's Cup defense boats, had died of typhoid fever in 1891 at the age of forty-two. Meanwhile, Nathanael Herreshoff had established himself as a rival to Burgess in designing and producing fast racing sloops. Herreshoff had designed and built *Vigilant,* which defended the cup in 1893. So absent competition from Burgess, it was no surprise that on behalf of the syndicate, C. Oliver Iselin again contracted with the Herreshoff Manufacturing Company on January 23, 1895, to design and build a new boat.

In response to the club's commission, Herreshoff set about drafting a new design employing the most advanced technology of the day. In many respects, *Defender* resembled the fastest British boats of the era. It was radically different from the Burgess products. *Defender* also differed from earlier boats from Herreshoff's own drafting table. For example, although his successful *Vigilant* design had used a centerboard, by 1895, Herreshoff favored boats that had deep fixed keels, and that is what he used on *Defender*. In fact, *Defender* was the first deep fixed-keel boat selected by the New York Yacht Club to defend the cup since *America*.

The design called for a relatively narrow beam and deep draft. It was to be 88.5 feet on the waterline. *Defender* spread 12,602 square feet of sail. Hull, spars and sails were all to be designed, developed and built by the Herreshoff Manufacturing Company.

Defender was to be a composite boat. Its hull, deck plates and deck beams were made of aluminum in order to minimize weight. From the waterline and down, it was plated with Tobin bronze—heavy, strong and corrosion-resistant. Frames were steel and its external ballast lead. *Defender* was designed and built for maximized speed and nothing else. The fact that it was built from different metals guaranteed that it wouldn't last more than a few racing seasons.

Metals in contact with different metals break down through a process termed galvanic corrosion. Throw in salt water, and the galvanic process is further complicated by oxidation. Aluminum touching bronze touching steel guaranteed a short life for *Defender*. Some writers like Brooks have suggested that Herreshoff was unaware of the galvanic corrosion problem he designed into *Defender*. This is highly unlikely. Galvanic corrosion was a phenomenon that had been well understood for centuries. As early as the sixteenth century, Britain's Royal Navy had observed that copper sheathing on warships accelerated corrosion of iron fittings below the waterline. Nathanael Herreshoff was a brilliant practical engineer. He had worked with metal in boats his entire career, and there is no question that he understood galvanic corrosion and the risks it added to a durable structure. Furthermore, it really didn't matter. He had been commissioned by the New York Yacht Club syndicate to build a fast boat capable of keeping the America's Cup bolted in place in the Tiffany showroom in 1895. Herreshoff was quoted as saying, "She had performed the mission, and that was all that she was constructed for. From the start, durability was put aside.[19] Of course, he knew he was designing a fast, short-lived boat—and fast it was.

BUILDING AND PREPARING DEFENDER

The contract cost of the yacht was $75,000 paid over six $12,500 installments. If the yard failed to deliver the boat before June 15, it would be charged a penalty of $100. On the other hand, if the yard delivered the boat before June 15, the syndicate agreed to pay a $1,000 bonus. The contract loosely specified a "racing sloop yacht, being No. 452 on the list of the Herreshoff Manufacturing Company." Contract dimensions were only approximate, which reflected Iselin's and the syndicates' confidence in Herreshoff's design capabilities. It was to be about 123 feet in extreme length—89 feet on the waterline, 23 feet at the extreme beam and 19 feet in draft. Her draft was so much greater than anything Herreshoff had turned out before that the yard had to build a new and deeper launching way to handle the new cutter.

The contract specified the materials for hull framing, deck framing, hull plating above and below the waterline and deck plating. The deck surface itself was made of select white pine. Spars were originally steel (including a telescoping topmast, a Herreshoff innovation) but were later switched to Oregon pine. Sails were included. It was to have removable berths for twenty-two crewmen below as well as four "water closets," two sinks and two seven-hundred-gallon copper tanks for fresh water. The crews' quarters had a galley with a range, cooking utensils, a sink, dish racks and dishes for the crew. In other words, it was to be a complete racing yacht built in six months and delivered for $75,000.[20]

Defender was launched on June 29, 1895. A large complement of Deer Isle crewmen had already arrived and went to work with the yard workers and subcontractors to get *Defender* ready. The Herreshoff yard subcontracted most big-boat rigging work to Charles Billman and Son (Boston), and the Deer Isle men worked alongside. Having the race crew work on setting up the rigging—bending sails on and outfitting the yacht to get it ready for sea—was sensible and not at all unusual. This was before the days of hyper-specialization in yacht design, construction, preparation and racing. Many of the men had construction and rigging experience, as they built, rigged and sailed boats at home or learned through work on merchant

The Herreshoff designed and built composite metal cutter *Defender* on an easy port tack in 1895. *Image © Mystic Seaport, #1951.15.1.*

vessels and yachts on which they'd served. In addition, having the race crew help prepare the yacht made practical sense. If equipment was lost, broken or required modification to optimize sailing performance, having

The Deer Isle crew hoisting *Defender*'s mainsail and bending on her foresails. All running rigging was handled by sheer manpower aboard *Defender*. *Image © Mystic Seaport, #1951.15.21.*

crewmen aboard during trials and the races themselves who were familiar with the boat's systems allowed such modifications and repairs to be made on the fly, minimizing any loss of time or position. These systems did break. For example, both *Defender* and *Columbia* suffered spar breakage, including snapped mainmasts, during trial races. *Defender* raced in the Goelet Cup race for sloops over the Block Island course against *Vigilant, Volunteer* and *Jubilee*. While leading off West Island, its hollow wooden gaff snapped in the middle, forcing it to retire. The Deer Isle men were ready to help when and where they could, thereby reducing the need to return the boat to the yard in Bristol for repairs or upgrades.

Defender's sea trials began on July 6, 1895, in Narragansett Bay. The first America's Cup race was scheduled for September 7. Hank Haff, his officers and the Deer Isle men had just over two months to get acquainted with the new boat, to tune its rigging and ballast and to gel into a high-performance and integrated racing team.

THE CHALLENGER

In June, Lord Dunraven's newest *Valkyrie* had been launched, and its sea trials began on June 21, 1895. Lawson wrote:

> *Valkyrie III was steel framed with American elm planking below the waterline and mahogany above.*
>
> *She was, unquestionably, England's speediest boat, and in turning to windward in light airs and smooth sea was as fast as any yacht afloat, Defender excepted. She was manned by an able crew of Wivenhoe men whose training in boat sailing sprung from the Essex coast fisheries. Her Captain, William Cranfield, and his assistant, Edward Sycamore, were both Wivenhoe men.*[21]

Valkyrie III was designed by George Watson and built by D. and W. Henderson and Co. in Glasgow, Scotland. Following its sea trials, it left the Clyde on July 27, 1895, jury-rigged as a North Sea ketch for the passage across the Atlantic.[22] It had forty-two crewmen and officers aboard, and their passage was a rough one. As reported in the *Times* of London:

> *Valkyrie's log shows that between July 31 and August 4, a hard gale prevailed, and the yacht labored heavily, shipping a great deal of water all over. Early on the morning of August 2, the wheel ropes and pin and the running tackle block were carried away. On August 3, the yacht had to lie to for several hours. On the 6th, the mizzen peak halyards, the topsail sheet, and the boom guy halyards were carried away. The mainsail was repaired on the 7th. On the 8th, the jib topsail sheet was carried away.*

The fact that *Valkyrie III* had to be sailed across the Atlantic to enter the race, whereas *Defender* could enjoy a relatively leisurely delivery from Rhode Island up Long Island Sound, reopened a recurring debate in America's Cup circles—was the requirement imposed by the New York Yacht Club that challengers must arrive for the races "on her own bottom" unfair? The design, construction and rigging requirements of a sailing vessel capable of making a safe transatlantic passage were (and still are) very different from those of a sailing vessel intended to simply sail fast around marks in coastal waters. *Valkyrie III*, appropriately jury-rigged, was a seaworthy boat, but the question was whether it was too heavy and slow as a result. Its crew also arrived in New

York exhausted by the long and difficult passage. With racing rig setup, tuning, racing sails to bend on and yacht hauling and cleaning ahead of them, gazing across at the new lightly constructed *Defender*, with its well-rested crew of Deer Isle men, must have been daunting for the Wivenhoe crew.

Regardless, with characteristic British understatement, on August 20, *Valkyrie III*'s helmsman Edward Sycamore told reporters that "he had been pleased with the boat. Asked if she had been strained in any way during the voyage, he replied, 'No indeed; I don't anticipate anything wrong; she behaved nobly.' Mr. Sycamore also informed the correspondent that the crew were in splendid health."

The British team claimed to be ready at this time of the event when the sporting spirit still prevailed. But that spirit would be lost soon enough.

THE *DEFENDER* TRIALS

The sea trials for the new *Defender* began early in July. As might have been expected with a new yacht built using cutting edge technology, trials began to reveal problems. First, it was a leaky boat. *Defender* was lightly built and heavily ballasted. Brooks wrote:

> *Herreshoff remarked to the syndicate for whom he had built her that he was especially proud of his use of aluminum. During her trials, however, it was rumored that the Defender was not a strong boat, and it was questioned whether her mast, under certain tensions, wouldn't go right through her hull. Manager Iselin vigorously denied the rumor.*[23]

Defender's hull structure used the most advanced but largely unproven metal technology of the 1890s. The engineering world was fascinated with metal at the time, particularly aluminum. Its uses and properties were still being explored, and it was considered a somewhat exotic structural material. The process that made aluminum purification inexpensive (and thereby launched the metal into widespread use) had been perfected only seven years before *Defender* was launched in Bristol. The first American aluminum company (the predecessor of Alcoa) had only recently been founded (in 1888). By employing aluminum—both alone and in combination with other advanced metals—Herreshoff was at the forefront of materials engineering.

Defender slipping past *Corsair*, J.P. Morgan's steam yacht. Morgan helped fund the *Defender* campaign and provided almost all of the funding for *Columbia* four years later. *Image © Mystic Seaport, Rosenfeld Collection, #B643. Photographer: James Burton.*

Steel was in a heyday. Its properties were well understood, and advancements in component ratios were well explored. Herreshoff had worked with steel for years in his steam-powered vessels. The Brooklyn Bridge, that marvel of slender steel roping and cables, had opened twelve years earlier. The Eiffel Tower, still today the most recognizable monument to structural metallurgy, was under construction in France and would open the Paris Exposition in 1899. However, it was the combination of materials that presented the difficulties for *Defender*. Its aluminum and bronze plates would have had differential thermal and tensile properties; in other words, they would expand, contract and flex at different rates and in different ways. The *New York Tribune* reported on July 9, 1895, that after sea trials:

> *The Defender strained some of her strengthening braces yesterday while on her second trial trip off the south end of Prudence Island. When she*

arrived at her anchorage in Bristol Harbor, it was discovered that the two steel pieces of piping that are bolted from the angle iron deck braces to the bilge brace stringers were bent and twisted out of shape on account of the great strain they were subject to in carrying the sails. The aluminum plates in that region did not show any indication of bending, but they must have been sprung somewhat to cause the steel braces to bend.

Holding a tight seal between the aluminum and bronze plates presented an engineering challenge, particularly in a heavy sea. If the *Defender* shipped significant amounts of water, thereby adding weight, it may have been difficult for it to maintain the same waterline overnight or through a four- or five-hour race. Could this fact alone have fed the ballast controversies that stormed across the *Defender-Valkyrie III* series later that summer?

Defender's initial trial races off Sandy Hook were held against the rejuvenated *Vigilant* (defender in 1893), *Volunteer* (defender in 1887) and one other defense hopeful, *Jubilee. Defender* was towed from its mooring off Iselin's home in New Rochelle down to New York and hauled out at Erie Basin (in Brooklyn near the present-day Redhook Pier and Brooklyn Cruise Terminal). There the crew went to work getting *Defender* into trial-racing form. As reported in the *New York World* on July 25, 1895:

The veil of secrecy which had surrounded and hidden Defender from the time the first plate of her keel was riveted had now been cast entirely aside. The beautiful yacht stands reveled in all the perfection of her symmetrical lines in the big Boston dry dock at Erie Basin, a feast for nautical eyes. At 4 o'clock this morning, there was unwonted activity up at Premium Point, New Rochelle Harbor, and the yacht's crew prepared for an early start. The tug Walter B. Flint passed a line [to Defender], and accompanied by the floating kitchen, bedroom, dining-room and store-house Hattie Palmer, the new bronze beauty was towed down the Sound and the East River to Robin's dock. As the water receded [in dry dock], the crew got to work in pontoons, plying their stiff brooms industriously to clean the side below the waterline.

Defender had been built with Spartan accommodations for the Deer Isle crew. Iselin had chartered the steam vessel *Hattie Palmer* to tend to *Defender's* needs, as well as the needs of its crew. In addition, once they learned that *Valkyrie III* had no such accommodations aboard, *Defender* was stripped of its basic comforts, leaving only the twenty pipe berths in the forecastle for

A conference below decks aboard *Columbia* in the summer of 1899. Both *Columbia* and *Defender* were Spartan below to save topside weight. Crewmen slept aboard on cots and pipe berths but stowed their bedding aboard the yacht tenders prior to each day's work. It would have been very difficult for illegal lead ballast shifting to be hidden from sight. *Image © Mystic Seaport, #1951.14.340.*

overnight use. The weight of the removed fixtures was offset by adding two tons of moveable lead ballast before the yachts were measured for their first race. *Hattie Palmer* was a converted tug fitted with an oversized deckhouse topped by a wheelhouse. It was commanded by a Captain Taylor and had a galley, dining area and bunkroom for some of the crew and ample storage on deck and below for equipment and supplies. Most crewmen slept aboard *Defender* but took their meals aboard *Hattie Palmer* throughout the Goelet Cup trials off Sandy Hook, the Drexel Cup races near Newport, the Astor Cup finals (again off Sandy Hook) that followed and the America's Cup competition itself. They would transfer cots and bedding to *Defender* each night, and re-stow them aboard *Hattie Palmer* each morning. They also used the tender as a workshop and storeroom. Suspected night work aboard the *Hattie Palmer* as it lay in its usual position alongside *Defender* on the night of September 6, 1895, would figure prominently in the testimonies of Lord Dunraven and his officers later in the year when they accused the Iselin team of peculiarities in *Defender*'s ballasting.

The August races for the Drexel Cup were particularly heated. Accidents happened, and the officers and crews were stretched to the limits of their sailing skill. *Vigilant* proved to be particularly aggressive, helmed by the young Charlie Barr. Charles Barr was the younger brother of Captain John Barr, who had distinguished himself sailing for Great Britain at the helm of *Thistle* in 1887. To quote Brooks writing of Charlie Barr, "A historian of the Cup matches called him 'probably the greatest skipper that ever trod the deck of a racing yacht, an aggressive and magnificent helmsman.'"[24]

Haff and his crew were up against a fast, proven and well-handled opponent. Protest and argument flared; however, the trial races were not without moments of chivalry. On August 6, 1895, E.A. Willard, owner of *Vigilant*, decided to withdraw his boat from the competition. His letter to the New York Yacht Club stated, "I have twice given way to *Defender* at the start of a race, when Vigilant clearly had the right of way, because I was unwilling to risk a collision which might have left America without a Cup defender."

Among the New Yorkers, most hoped that Herreshoff's new boat would be selected to defend the cup. In the aggressive racing during the summer of 1895, Willard and the club were mindful of the fact that under club rules, any competitor participating in a club-sponsored race regatta that was involved in more than one protest could be banned from subsequent club regattas, including the America's Cup races. Lawson wrote:

> *Mr. Willard, owner of Vigilant, in one trial race vs. Defender lodged a protest and lost. He believed he was fouled again in a second race but abstained from protesting as under Club rules, a boat twice the subject of protest would be barred from further racing in the season. He withheld his second protest to ensure that Defender would not be barred from the Cup races later in the same season.*[25]

Also on August 6, Willard sent a second letter to the club unreservedly offering *Vigilant* up as a trial horse for *Defender* and its crew to prepare for the far more important priority: the America's Cup races against Dunraven's *Valkyrie III*.

The Drexel Cup having been decided by Willard's withdrawal, *Defender* was taken to the Herreshoff yard in Bristol for a rigging refit. On August 9, *Defender* grounded on a sand bar in Narragansett Bay but came off uninjured.[26] Later that month, it was back in New York getting ready for the trial finals.

On August 20, *Defender* met *Vigilant* again off Sandy Hook. John Jacob Astor put up a trophy for the race. *Defender*'s mast buckled during the race, and it was again sent to Bristol for re-rigging. It shipped a new mast of Oregon pine fabricated in Boston, longer and stronger than the discarded steel spar. Its topmast was also of Oregon pine, but it shipped a hollow gaff and boom made of steel. The Deer Isle crew pitched in to help the yard workers and rigging contractor return *Defender* to racing form.

The British watched the *Defender-Vigilant* trials off Sandy Hook closely. Even with its new wooden mast, *Defender*'s light rigging continued to present problems. The London *Times* correspondent reported in late August that when *Defender*'s topmast shroud had sprung (foreshadowing the broken shroud caused by *Defender*'s brush with *Valkyrie* at the start of the second cup race), the British observers were keen to criticize *Defender*'s seaworthiness:

> *No official account of yesterday's mishap to the Defender has been published, but those on board say that the steel band on the mast just below the hounds to which the shrouds* [probably spreaders] *are attached slipped. The shrouds were therefore slackened, and Captain Haff thought that the mast would have been in some danger if the Defender had gone on. The wind had freshened during the first round, and the sea had grown heavier, but there was nothing to affect a yacht in good condition. "I fail to understand," says Mr. Glennie, who is here as Lord Dunraven's friend, "why a breeze should prove too much for the Defender's stability." He thinks her a grand boat but is surprised at her lightness. This is the third breakdown of the Defender and the third race she has lost from defects of construction, or perhaps, from ill-luck.*

The public and, consequently, the newspaper interest in the trial races were extraordinary. The *New York World* arranged for a reporter to ascend in a balloon tethered to a Sandy Hook beach. This extraordinary arrangement was described by the newspaper on August 19, 1895, under the headline "Reporting by Balloon":

> *Interest in the trial races for the selection of the defender of the America's Cup, to be sailed tomorrow morning, is hardly secondary to that displayed in the coming cup races themselves. As in previous races, "The Evening World" has neglected no preparations for furnishing the public with the details of the trials while they are progressing. The facilities afforded by special tugs, carrier-pigeons, special wires, &c., will again be supplemented, as in the recent races, by a captive balloon, from which an expert, who is a sailor newspaper man and telegraph reporter, will describe the race as seen from his lofty perch, over a wire leading directly into "The Evening World" office.*

The following day, the balloon-based reporting adventure was declared a success by the *Evening World*. The newspaper claimed "aerial reporting is no

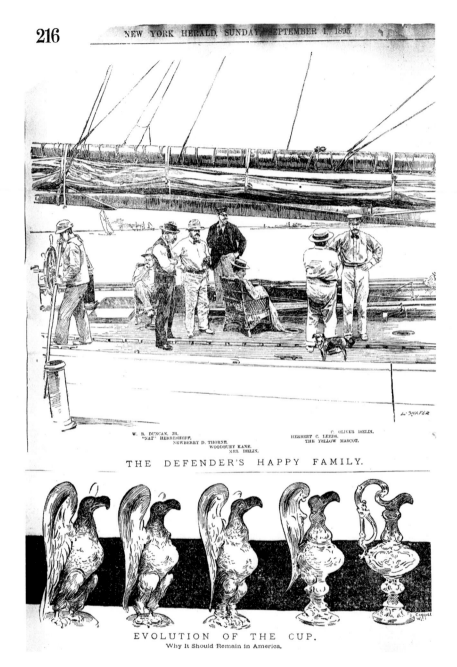

THE DEFENDER'S HAPPY FAMILY.

W. R. DUNCAN, JR.
"NAT" HERRESHOFF.
NEWBERRY D. THORNE.
WOODBURY KANE.
MRS. ISELIN.

C. OLIVER ISELIN.
HERBERT C. LEEDS.
THE YELLOW MASCOT.

EVOLUTION OF THE CUP.
Why It Should Remain in America.

The September 1, 1895 *New York Herald* is suggesting that the original Queen's Cup would forever be the America's Cup in this amusing sketch. In the upper panel, Hope Goddard Iselin is shown seated in the wicker deck chair surrounded by the *Defender* afterguard. The Deer Isle crewman fending off the launch with a pole is unidentified. *Courtesy of the New York Yacht Club.*

longer an experiment. It is an assured success." As before, *Defender* was sailed by Hank Haff and his all-Deer Isle crew. *Vigilant* was handled by Charlie Barr. During the Astor Cup series, *Valkyrie III* shadowboxed with its future competitor by sailing alongside *Defender* and *Vigilant*, albeit always at a safe and discrete distance. Its skipper and Wivenhoe crew began to see that once *Defender*'s rigging problems had been solved, it was indeed a very fast and well-handled boat.

The first Astor Cup race was held on August 20. *Vigilant* led at the start, but *Defender* seemed to be the faster boat and had passed *Vigilant* by the time they approached the first mark. It was then that Haff and the crew noticed that *Defender*'s rig was failing. The crew stood by, awaiting Haff's order to jibe, and it didn't come. Instead, as it passed the mark six minutes and thirty seconds ahead of *Vigilant*, Haff had the men hold the same tack, and it bore off the wind, seemingly reaching off the course. They had noticed that its shrouds were loosening, and rather than risk a catastrophic mast failure like they'd experienced in July off of Newport, they retired from the race altogether. The race was awarded to *Vigilant*.

Generously, the race committee postponed the next race for a week to give Haff and his team time to make repairs. On August 30, the two yachts met again, and that day's races left no doubt which was the faster of the two. In a heavy breeze, *Defender* proved to be faster both windward and when running downwind. In a rare mention of the crewmen working aboard *Defender*, the newspapers wrote about their sail handling, believing (likely correctly) that Haff and his men deliberately slowed *Defender* so as to not give the observers aboard *Valkyrie III* an accurate measure of its speed. The *World* reported on August 30, 1895:

> *It was but a succession of tacks to the outer mark, Defender gaining at every jump. Haff may have luffed a little more than was necessary nearing the stake boat, for English eyes watched him from Valkyrie, which had stood towards the Long Island shore but had not followed the racers. Her Desert Island [sic] crew made no haste to set the spinnaker after rounding for the run home, flat down wind, but took things in a leisurely fashion, as though her commanders were certain that Vigilant could not possibly overcome the big lead.*

On August 31, Iselin received word that *Defender* was officially chosen to represent the New York Yacht Club in the America's Cup races against the challenger from Great Britain, Lord Dunraven's *Valkyrie III*. However, as noted by Jerome Brooks, in retrospect, many came to wish that these races had never happened.

THE 1895 AMERICA'S CUP RACES

The 1895 America's Cup races were the most controversial and stressful in the long and tumultuous history of this event. There were a number of specific reasons why, but mainly the catastrophe of 1895 arose from a clash of cultures, as the traditional, honor-bound and self-assured aristocracy represented by Lord Dunraven and his entourage collided with the publicity-sensitive, cutthroat, win-at-nearly-any-cost competitors of New York represented by Iselin and his syndicate. In this case, the New York culture won. The New Yorkers didn't just beat Dunraven; they annihilated him.

Thirty-five men from Deer Isle stood unblinking in the harsh spotlight of this controversy. They were required to act a part that they'd never expected. They had been recruited by men they knew and liked: George Conant, their neighbor; Fred Weed, a man whose seagoing career was of the highest order and one to which most sailing Deer Islers aspired; and Hank Haff, the affable and extraordinarily well qualified veteran of the New York yacht-racing scene. *Defender*'s Deer Isle crewmen were hired to sail Herreshoff's big, new metal cutter, to sail it fast and well, to obey orders and to stay sober. For that, they were well paid and given travel, food, new rubber shoes and a uniform. Instead, what they got was one race against the British in which they later were accused of cheating, one race at the start of which their rigging was hooked and damaged by their opponent before they'd crossed the starting line and a third race for which they showed up ready and able to sail only to see their petulant competitor poke his nose over the line and then sail back to his mooring in a huff. Finally, they endured a months-long ordeal in which in order to preserve their personal honor as well as any prospect of future employment in yachts anywhere on the eastern seaboard, they had to sign legal affidavits. Fifteen men even had to travel to New York over the Christmas holidays to testify in person to help prove that they had neither seen, heard nor performed any action prohibited by the rules of the America's Cup. The *Defender* crew from Deer Isle performed well enough as sailors to beat *Vigilant*, *Volunteer*, *Jubilee* and *Valkyrie III* on the water when given a clean race. Perhaps more importantly, each one did his duty, under

A sketch from the September 7, 1895 *New York World* showing John Hyslop measuring the waterline length of *Defender*. Waterline length controversy would ultimately ruin what was left of Lord Dunraven's sporting reputation in the United States and would eventually force him to retire from competitive yacht racing. *Courtesy of the New York Yacht Club.*

oath, and said the right thing (and the same thing), allowing Iselin to win again in the private court proceedings that followed.

On the afternoon of September 6, 1895, the tug *Wallace B. Flint* towed *Defender* into the dry dock at Erie Basin. Herreshoff, Iselin, Haff and his entire Deer Isle racing crew were all aboard. When the towline was cast off, the Deer Islers threw lines, and when they had been secured, warped *Defender* into position alongside *Valkyrie III*. The crew was not there to clean her underbody after the water had been pumped out of the dock. They were there to be measured. All of the men and their sailing gear, even their clay pipes, had to be aboard so that *Defender*'s load waterline could be measured as accurately as possible in the calm water of the enclosed basin. Haff and the officers instructed the men to sit quietly and as close to the big cutter's centerline as possible. If the weight wasn't distributed properly or if they were to shift about, then the waterline measurement would be inaccurate, and *Defender* might be assigned an incorrect time adjustment in the forthcoming race with *Valkyrie III*. The men complied, and at about 1:30 p.m., the official New York Yacht Club measurers, led by John Hyslop, went to work measuring *Defender*'s deck and waterline using the identical and exact methods he had employed on *Valkyrie III* earlier in the day.

Somewhat surprisingly to the British, *Defender* was measured twice. Once Herreshoff learned that Hyslop had measured *Valkyrie III*'s waterline at eighty-nine feet, six inches, a few inches longer than *Defender*'s, he ordered three or four additional tons of lead to be loaded into *Defender* from the *Hattie Palmer*. The Deer Islers went to work transferring the heavy lead pigs or ingots from one vessel across to the other and stowed them below decks aboard the race boat. *Defender* sank lower in the water with the added ballast, and her waterline was remeasured. The process was hard work and required several hours.

Evidently, Herreshoff thought that with more weight and a longer waterline, *Defender* would be faster. He also thought, correctly, that even with an equal waterline length, *Defender* would still retain a rating advantage over *Valkyrie III* due to the latter's significantly larger sail area. Hyslop compliantly remeasured, and the impatient crew was finally released for "slops," the term Haff used for supper. A few of the crew stripped off their shirts and plunged into the Erie Basin water, welcoming a cooling swim after a long and hot afternoon despite the filth of New York's East River.

This last-minute shifting of ballast might have raised suspicions among the British—and Lord Dunraven in particular. Herreshoff was always working to tune and improve *Defender*. There was no reason he shouldn't have added moveable ballast, provided that the last measurement of the boat included the exact ballast it would carry in the race the following day. What may be most noteworthy, however, is that Herreshoff and Iselin were clearly convinced that more weight meant a faster boat. As we will discuss later, during the December testimony, the American side relied on the position that more weight did *not* mean a faster boat and that if Dunraven's accusations of more ballast being added the night of September 6 after official measurements were taken were true, that *Defender* would have been *slower*. Therefore, maintained the Americans, why would anybody try to do it? This contradiction was never addressed in testimony.

At seven o'clock the following morning, Quartermasters Irving Barbour, John Billings, Gardie Greene and John Staples rousted the men from their cots and berths in the *Defender* forecastle. The removable cots and all bedding that had not been aboard during measurement—a hazard in a race anyway—were stowed aboard the *Hattie Palmer*. The men and officers sat down in the messroom to a quiet breakfast served by William Hardy. After the sea trials and all of the trial races off Newport and Sandy Hook, the crew was ready for the big race. It was time to show the British just how fast their big metal cutter was. More to the point, they wanted to show the British, and the world, how a crew of working men from a small island off the coast of Maine could sail just as well as or even better than the yacht-racing pros from Wivenhoe, England.

THE FIRST RACE: SATURDAY, SEPTEMBER 7, 1895

On September 8, 1895, front-page headlines on the *San Francisco Call* blared, "Captain Haff Guided the American Single-Sticker to Victory." The first America's Cup race was national news.

During the week before the America's Cup races, *Defender* was brought in to Erie Basin in Brooklyn for final race preparations. The Deer Isle hands scrubbed its bronze underbody, and a few of them took up brushes to help subcontractors repaint its topsides. *Defender* was no longer white; it was now a light blue. Most models and paintings of *Defender* show the ship in its more attractive white livery, but when it raced *Valkyrie III*, its hull was blue.

After revelry at 7:00 a.m. on Saturday, September 7, the foredeck hands on *Defender* cast off the mooring at the Brooklyn Navy Yard. It had a long tow astern of the *Wallace B. Flint* to the south through the Verrazano Narrows and out into Raritan Bay and the Atlantic Ocean. The navy yard mooring had been leased by Iselin for the summer. Once clear of land, at 8:50 a.m., the Deer Isle crew gang-hoisted *Defender*'s enormous mainsail and gaff and set the working jib. The towline was cast off, and the sparkling Herreshoff cutter was once again underway.

It was a seven-nautical-mile sail from the narrows to the starting area marked by the Sandy Hook lightship. The wind was five knots from the southwest, and seas were small. It looked to be a light-air race day, conditions that would seem to favor the aluminum-and-steel American boat over its heavier mahogany-and-elm rival. However, *Valkyrie III* could carry more sail, so Haff and the Deer Isle crew tried to gauge their speed against the British boat and her disciplined crew from Wivenhoe.

At around 9:30 a.m., the Deer Isle mastmen went aloft and set the club topsail, that distinctive high sail that fills the triangular space between the topmast and mainsail gaff. Charlie Scott, later to retire from yachting to operate the family ferry business running between Seargentville on the mainland and Scott's Landing on North Deer Isle, worked one hundred feet above the deck to get the topsail set correctly. The press commented that *Defender*'s sails looked to be in perfect form. Herreshoff and the Deer Isle crew had worked hard to tune the rig and re-cut the sails so that *Defender* would be in top racing form when it finally met *Valkyrie III* on the racecourse.

The spectator fleet was out early and in force. Steamers began loading passengers at Brooklyn, Manhattan, Staten Island, Navasink, New Jersey and elsewhere. Dunraven was concerned, and rightly so. The excursion fleet

A close-up view of mastmen at work aboard *Defender*. Falls from these heights were uncommon but did occur. The Deer Islers were accustomed to this risky work from their service aboard other sailing yachts and coastal schooners. © *Mystic Seaport, #1951.15.32.*

repeatedly interfered with the races. Captains of observing steamers would often disregard any efforts at control. After all, they were being paid to give their customers a good view of the competition, often in limited visibility. Brooks wrote:

> *The first race, September 7, 1895, was attended by the hugest pleasure-boat fleet yet seen. Its presence gave the contestants and the regatta committee no pleasure. On the more than 200 steamers and other craft which crowded the*

course were an estimated 60,000 paying passengers. This was far beyond the common-sense bounds of safety for many of the vessels. Twenty steam yachts had been assigned by the New York Yacht Club to try to keep the course clear enough for the helmsmen on both racers to see where they were going.[27]

Lord Dunraven had asked, both prior to and even during the races, to shift the course to a less accessible venue. It was a hazy day, and visibility was limited, so they were further motivated to stay as close to the race boats as possible. It was near pandemonium complicated by the fact that due to the wind direction, the race committee re-laid the course only a couple of hours before the race began, and the excursion boats rushed to take up new positions, completely overwhelming the dozen course control boats chartered by the New York Yacht Club to keep the course clear. During this first race, the steamers were an annoyance. During the second, an errant excursion vessel would prove to be the race's undoing.

The warning gun sounded at 12:15 p.m. from the deck of the anchored race committee boat *Luckenbach*. Aboard *Defender*, the bowsprit crew, mastmen, portside trimmers and starboard trimmers were all ready. Each quartermaster commanded his team of men, with whom each had sailed, worked and, in some cases, grown up with on their downeast island. After three months of working and living together aboard *Defender*, they had developed that sixth sense of anticipating each other's moves and for routine matters worked seamlessly together under Hank Haff's command and C. Oliver Iselin's careful watch.

They had two beloved mascots aboard. One was a yellow dog named Sandy, whose origin is lost to history. The other, whose name justifiably has remained prominent in America's Cup lore, was C. Oliver's wife, Hope Goddard Iselin. Rated as "timekeeper" on *Defender*, Hope Iselin was the first woman to sail aboard a competitor during the races. She was beloved by the crew, and as evidenced by her many photographs reproduced in this volume, she was also a gifted amateur photographer. Using the new Brownie camera during the *Columbia* series, she captured for the first time images of the crew at work aboard a defense boat during America's Cup races.

Because of the light air, there was only moderate pre-race maneuvering. Both boats executed several tacks and jibes in preparation for the upwind start. Captain Cranfield of Wivenhoe bested Captain Haff of Islip in these maneuvers, and when the starting gun sounded at 12:20 p.m., *Valkyrie III* crossed the line four seconds ahead of *Defender*, both boats close hauled on starboard tack. It was a clean start.

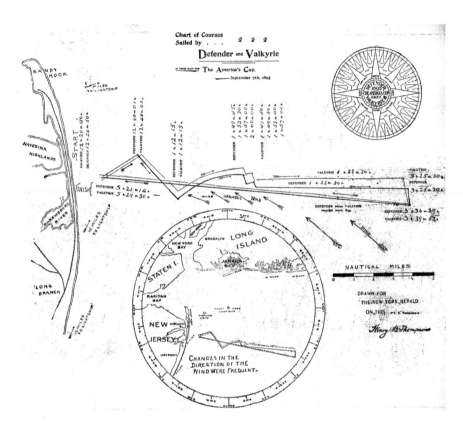

The boats close reached to the northeast for about twenty minutes. Haff gave the command to tack. As *Defender*'s helm went to lee, it turned into the eye of the breeze, and just as they'd done one hundred times before, the portside crew cast off the jib, staysail sheets and running backstay and the starboard side crew hauled away. The enormous boom that hung out over the stern by twenty feet swung across the deck as the starboard side trimmed like madmen and sheeted the foresails home. Seconds later, Captain Cranfield ordered the same maneuver aboard *Valkyrie III*, and it swung over to the port tack to cover. Thirty minutes later, Haff ordered another tack, and this time, the starboard crew cast off while the port side trimmed. Cranfield covered again. At that point in the race, sailing conditions began to change. The wind gradually freshened and clocked ten degrees to the south. The boats were still not able to sail directly to the mark, but the direct line to the mark lay closer to their heading. The freshening breeze also began to erase the advantage that *Valkyrie III* derived from its larger sail area (with about two thousand extra square feet of sail, it could match the lighter-hulled *Defender* with greater sail power.) But as the breeze freshened, its large sail area began to be less of an advantage and more of a liability. Haff sensed this. After forty minutes on the starboard tack, he ordered another tack. *Defender* swung to a southeast, heading on port tack. Cranfield covered as he had before. Four minutes later, Haff tacked again. Cranfield again covered. What Haff had discovered was that *Defender* and its crew could turn through a tack and accelerate out of the maneuver more quickly than *Valkyrie III*. So he tacked again and then again. After these moves, Haff had *Defender* on a starboard tack heading close to the lay line and had pulled even with *Valkyrie III*. They were now windward of the British and able to control the race. Haff saw for himself the result of Herreshoff's genius as the breeze freshened even more. With its deep ballast and light rig, *Defender* could not only match *Valkyrie III's* speed, she could sail closer to the wind. *Defender* pointed higher, and that made the difference.

Opposite, top: The *New York Herald* published the course chart with times at each maneuver and mark for the first race between *Defender* and *Valkyrie III*, sailed on September 7, 1895. It was to be the only clean race of the series and was won by *Defender*. *Courtesy of the New York Yacht Club.*

Opposite, bottom: Foredeck crew aboard *Defender*. The size of the foresails the Deer Isle crews were working with is evident in this striking photograph. *Image © Mystic Seaport, Rosenfeld Collection, #Y421C. Photographer: Charles Edwin Bolles.*

The foredeck crew on *Defender* running up a spinnaker in stops. Once aloft, the sheet and guy would be trimmed, breaking the stops and hopefully resulting in a full and pulling chute. *Image © Mystic Seaport, Rosenfeld Collection, #Y834A. Photographer: Charles Edwin Bolles.*

Almost exactly two hours into the race, both boats had to make one more tack to the south to round the windward mark. *Defender* rounded first, having sailed a substantially shorter windward leg due to its ability to point. It was around the mark three minutes ahead.

The Deer Isle foredeck crew was frantically at work at this point. It was time to set the enormous spinnaker for the fifteen-mile downwind leg back to the west and the finish line. The Americans chose a stopped launch; the sail was run up in stops and was broken out once the head of the sail had reached the mainmast truck. The masthead team was aloft readying the balloon topsail, a billowy version of the topsail that had performed well on the upwind leg. This was dangerous work. Sailors aloft were roped in, but if they'd slipped or lost their one-handed grip, they were greeted by a long fall and violent arrest by their harness. Bones might break, and bruises were guaranteed. Fortunately, the spinnaker and balloon topsail sets went as practiced, and within minutes, *Defender* was tearing downwind. *Valkyrie III,* partly by British tradition and partly because it was losing the race, used a free set; its spinnaker went up unstopped in the lee of its mainsail. It worked, but not well enough. *Valkyrie III* fell farther behind. *Defender* tore across the finish line with an elapsed time of five hours, twenty-one minutes and fourteen seconds. *Valkyrie III* crossed with a time of five hours, twenty-nine minutes and thirty seconds. In addition, because of its larger sail area, *Valkyrie III* had to award time to *Defender,* so after correction, *Defender* had defeated the challenger by eight minutes and forty-nine seconds—a clear and convincing victory. The *San Francisco Call* captured the scene:

> *When the Defender sailed proudly over the finish line, she was given a tremendous ovation. Whistles were tooted long and loud and cannon boomed, and the many thousand excursionists shouted themselves hoarse in exultation over the gallant American boat's victory. On the Defender, the gentlemen all shook hands with Mr. Iselin, who stood on the companionway with a beaming countenance. Woodbury Kane danced a jig, waved his arms windmill fashion, and behaved like an overjoyful schoolboy. Mr. Leeds hugged Mr. Iselin, and all hands seemed to drop decorum and give way to hilarity.*

It must have been a great relief to the men from Deer Isle. They had, in a single thirty-mile race, proven that they not only could handle the job but that they could do it well. They had more than matched their British competitors.

After this first race, all was well in the press. The public mood was pleasant on both sides of the Atlantic. Good sportsmanship still prevailed. The *Times* of London reported:

The comments of the New York papers this morning on the Defender's victory are couched in a tone of moderation. One leading journal, the New York Times, remarks that every American yachtsman would be pleased to see the Valkyrie win two races out of five. The good humor of a first success is visible in the press, but Lord Dunraven's popularity is such that nobody wishes to exult over his defeat.

Unfortunately, the goodwill would not last long. Ahead of challenger and defender lay the next race—an event that would be the beginning of the public undoing of Lord Dunraven.

THE SECOND RACE: TUESDAY, SEPTEMBER 10, 1895, AND "THE FOUL"

Tuesday, September 10 dawned warm and humid. The crew was rousted from their berths at the usual 7:00 a.m. and after breakfast stowed their gear aboard the *Hattie Palmer*. Both *Defender* and *Valkyrie III* had moored overnight inside the horseshoe harbor at the end of Sandy Hook. *Defender* had a short tow out to the Sandy Hook lightship. By 9:30 a.m., sails were raised and the crews were in the final stages of race preparation.

At about 10:00 a.m., the race committee raised the signal on the *Luckenbach* indicating that the race would be sailed over the No. 2 course, a triangular course with three ten-mile legs. Further signaling showed that the start would be windward to the south, then northeast on a broad reach, then westward on a closer reach back to the lightship and the finish. Marks were to be left to port.

The breeze began to stir and was blowing six knots when the first warning gun was fired at 10:50 a.m. This time, the pre-race jockeying was more spirited. As the *New York Times* reported, "The two graceful racing machines…moved about as if on pivots, sparring for position in anticipation of the next signal." The Deer Isle and Wivenhoe crews were working hard, thirty-two men taking commands from quartermasters who instantly relayed orders from Haff on the American boat and Cranfield aboard the British. Captain Sycamore was at *Valkyrie III*'s tiller. The enormous cutters were so close that at times crewmen could hear the shouted commands from the other boat despite the rush of the water, the hum of the wind and the bangs and groans of the rigging.

The final warning gun was fired at 10:55 a.m. The two yachts came about and sailed away from the starting line, attempting to position optimally for the start. The skipper of the excursion steamer *City of Yorktown* had at just the wrong moment decided to improve his view of the impending start and steamed directly across the path between the contestants about six hundred yards before the starting line. As the two boats jibed and began what their helmsmen hoped would be a perfectly timed and full-speed windward start, there was the *Yorktown* directly ahead. Helmsman Sycamore had maneuvered *Valkyrie III* slightly to windward of *Defender*. It was a good position to be in, as he could blanket *Defender*'s breeze, slow it down and, perhaps, cross the line in the lead. However, the *Yorktown* was steaming from left to right directly across his bow. Sycamore was able to head up and pass to windward of the errant steamer, but Haff and *Defender* had to pass to leeward and astern. As they emerged from the *Yorktown* encounter, Sycamore fell off the wind to regain speed but avoid crossing the line too soon. Haff, to leeward and with the right of way, held his course.

It was then that a shackle on the aft end of *Valkyrie III*'s boom hit *Defender*'s starboard rigging. A *New York Herald* reporter saw the incident, and on September 11, the newspaper printed his account:

> *The Defender was close-hauled by the wind on the starboard tack, and the Valkyrie was coming to the line a little freer. Captain Haff would not give way and held his course. The Valkyrie, with sheets lifted a bit, bore down on him, and just as both were crossing the line, the Valkyrie luffed, and as the main sheet was being taken in the after end of the boom got caught in the starboard topmast shroud of the Defender and pulled it out of the spreader.*

Defender's starboard topmast shroud was slack, and its fully loaded topmast was bending dangerously over its port leeward side. Haff reacted immediately and turned *Defender* hard to starboard and into the wind. Over the booming din of the enormous luffing canvas sails, he shouted orders to Charlie Scott and the mast team. Six Deer Isle men, probably Scott and five others, leaped to the rigging and shot up the enormous mast. The *Herald* reported:

> *She had to heave to, and the topmast shroud was set in a cleat in the spreader. The crew then put a tackle on the topmast shroud and set it up, and this lost the Defender nearly 2 mins. While she was being nursed in getting the topmast shroud set up, the Valkyrie had a good lead. The snapping of the shroud out of the spreader caused the springing of the*

Defender on the right, *Valkyrie III* on the left near the committee boat *Luckenbach*. This photograph was taken five seconds after "The Foul" occurred on September 10, 1895, and was one of several used by the race committee to determine the validity of C. Oliver Iselin's protest. The committee ruled in favor of Iselin, and although *Valkyrie III* won the race on the course, it was almost caught by a jury-rigged *Defender* after the Deer Isle crew arranged a temporary fix to the slack topmast shroud aloft. *Courtesy of Beken Ltd. Cowes, United Kingdom.*

> *topmast, and before Defender got away, the Valkyrie had gained over a minute and a half by the accident.*

Haff determined that *Defender* could make the line on starboard tack, brought her around and with the healthy portside shroud now to windward and supporting its topmast, was able to get *Defender* across the start line. Iselin set a protest flag showing his belief that the collision with *Valkyrie III* was a foul. The flag was acknowledged by a gun from the *Luckenbach*.

Remarkably, *Defender* lost virtually no time with this luffing maneuver. It crossed the start line only one minute and two seconds behind. However, this was the windward leg of the thirty-mile, three-sided course, each leg ten miles long. Eventually, *Defender* would have to come about, re-exposing its slack starboard shroud to a huge load. Without some form of repair, the topmast would snap once Haff tacked. The mast crew was hard at work. The masthead men furled the topsail to ease the load on the topmast. The foredeck crew had furled the jib topsail as well. Several worked at the throat of the topmast attempting to strengthen it with wood and straps. Another pair worked to get the shroud back in working order. Grasping the slack but working wire shroud, a crewman eased out on to the spreader and hooked the wire farther out on the shroud. While this was happening, *Defender* was footing off well to the east of the direct line to the windward mark. Once the jury-rigged shroud was in place, Haff had no choice but to tack. He gingerly turned the yacht through the eye of the wind and back on the starboard tack, again exposing the displaced shroud and strained topmast to the weight of the wind. The rig held. He then ordered the topsail to be unfurled. As the big triangular sail was set, the topmast strained and bent, but still it held. That was enough. Haff nursed *Defender* toward the windward mark, and much to the delight of Haff and Iselin, by the time it rounded the mark, *Defender* had stayed close enough to *Valkyrie III* to still have a chance. They were only three minutes and fifty seconds behind.

As *Defender* turned the mark and went over to the other tack, Haff ordered the crew to crowd on all sail. The injured shroud was now to leeward and taking no strain. By the second mark and the turn for home downwind, *Defender* had gained seventeen seconds. The crew set the balloon topsail and spinnaker, and the injured *Defender* roared toward the finish, always gaining on *Valkyrie III*. It made up substantial time and crossed just one minute and sixteen seconds after the British yacht. It was not enough. Even with its favorable correction, *Defender* was forty-seven seconds behind *Valkyrie III*. For the first time since 1871, a British yacht had won an America's Cup race. But was the result to stand?

What the *Herald* reporter, the officers and crew aboard *Defender*, the committee boat and at least one photographer clearly saw was that *Valkyrie III* had committed a foul. Lord Dunraven did not agree. He felt strongly that his yacht had won the race. Because of the complications created by the *Yorktown*'s blunder across the starting area, Dunraven believed Sycamore had been forced off his line and that the collision was unavoidable. For Dunraven, this was but another example of interference by the unruly spectator fleet and another demonstration of the New York Yacht Club's inability to control it. Furthermore, he believed that Haff had deliberately turned *Defender* closer to the wind, thereby colliding with *Valkyrie III* as it was executing an avoidance maneuver. None of these views were corroborated by eyewitness or photographic evidence, but Dunraven was certain that he was right.

Echoing his perspective on crowd control, after the entire series had come to its ignominious end, on September 13, the *Times* of London wrote:

> *There is, indeed, a possibility that the result of the recent races may induce the Cup Committee to agree to an alteration in the conditions in which the match is sailed. If they would assent in substance to Lord Dunraven's proposal, that the races should be held where clear water could be assured, we do not doubt that either Lord Dunraven himself or some other British challenger would speedily test the powers of American builders and yachtsmen once again. They attempted the impossible task of controlling a mob of excursionists without adequate means, and in despite of fair warning. The consequence has been the complete failure of a meeting on which high hopes were fixed on both sides of the Atlantic.*

However, the New York Yacht Club Race Committee disagreed. During the evening of September 10, the committee met, reviewed the evidence, upheld the *Defender*'s protest and under section II of its racing rule 16, awarded the second race to *Defender*. Lord Dunraven was incensed.

The following day, Iselin wrote to the race committee offering to re-sail the race. His offer was politely but firmly refused. The committee decision was final. Iselin wrote to Dunraven as well, making the same offer, and received a somewhat chilly reply. Dunraven pointed out that the committee had made its decision, that a re-sail was pointless and that had Iselin believed that there was any question of whether *Valkyrie III* had fouled *Defender*, Iselin would not have set his protest flag. Dunraven continued to insist that Sycamore had been within the rules when he bore down on *Defender*, that *Defender* had "hardened up" to cause the collision and that the unruly spectator fleet had been the cause all along. The club's failure to control the mob was unacceptable.

That night, Lord Dunraven sat down to write a letter to the New York Yacht Club America's Cup Committee. It was also released to the press. This letter marked the end of the press' favorable treatment of the Irish aristocrat. Dunraven wrote:

> *Gentlemen: It is with great reluctance that I write to inform you that I decline to sail the Valkyrie anymore under the circumstances that have prevailed in the last two races, and for the following reasons.*

First—To attempt to start two such large vessels in such confined space and among moving steamers and tugboats is, in my opinion, exceedingly dangerous, and I will no further risk the lives of my men or the ship.

Second—At the start of the first race, the crowding was so great that we could not see the mark boat and could not tell when we were near the line; and we were much hampered by steamers, especially on the race home.

Today on the reach home, eight or nine steamers were to the windward of me, and, what was worse, a block of steamers were steaming level with me and close under my lee. I sailed nearly the whole distance in tumbling, broken water, in the heavy wash of these steamers.

To race under these conditions is, in my opinion, absurd, and I decline to submit to them again.

I would remind your committee that, foreseeing the trouble that might occur, I urged upon them the desirability of sailing off Marblehead or some locality other than New York bay and that they refused to do so. At the same time, I would testify to my full belief that your committee have done everything in their power to prevent overcrowding. It is impossible to keep a course free from causes of exceptional danger and clear enough to assure the probability that the result of the match will be decided according to the relative merits of the competing vessels.

The committee and the press were not moved. The general view was that *Defender* had suffered from the same interferences and attentions. There was no evidence of the spectator fleet interfering more with the British yacht than the American. While Dunraven may have been correct, his letter came across to the yacht club and the American public as complaints from a sorry loser.

Not yet knowing what would happen in the foul deliberations, the *Defender* crew and riggers worked late into the night and next day to reset the sprung starboard shroud and replace the damaged topmast. As there wasn't time to produce a new spar in Bristol and ship it to New York, they had to borrow a topmast from *Colonia*. The solution worked, and by Wednesday, September 11, they had *Defender* back into racing form.

On Thursday morning, September 12, *Defender* and its crew went through their usual routines and arrived at the starting area ready to race. The committee boat *Luckenbach* showed signals indicating that a race indeed would take place and that the yachts should make ready. *Valkyrie III* had arrived as well, but instead of Cranfield engaging Haff in the lively pre-start maneuvers both looked forward to, under Dunraven's orders, he held it in stays to one side of the start line under main and staysail alone. The starting gun sounded, and *Defender* crossed with racing canvas set and drawing. *Valkyrie III*, however, merely nudged across the start line. Dunraven broke out the New York Yacht Club burgee. *Valkyrie III* then came about, went back over the line and retired from the race. Haff dutifully sailed *Defender* around the thirty-mile course alone in a light breeze and haze, finishing within the required six-hour maximum time. Horns sounded, flags waved and handshakes were passed, but with far less jubilation than seen after the first race, which had been cleanly sailed and clearly won. What celebration there was occurred without a vanquished opponent anywhere in sight. The 1895 America's Cup races fizzled to an end.

Dunraven retired to his hotel and refused to speak with the press. After a few days, he boarded W.K. Vanderbilt's private yacht *Valiant* and departed for a five-week stay in Newport. He quietly sailed for England on September 26.

Lord Dunraven had failed to understand the nature of the contest he had entered. He mistakenly believed that the 1895 America's Cup was a sporting contest among wealthy and largely amateur gentlemen. He was incorrect. What the America's Cup had become was a media event, in many respects a precursor of twenty-first-century professional sports, including the America's Cup races of today. The America's Cup was becoming a creature of the news. For example, the flamboyant James Gordon Bennett Jr., New York Yacht Club member, commodore (1884–85) and, in his yacht *Henrietta*, winner of a transatlantic yacht race, owned the *New York Herald*. Bennett was a master at creating events that helped sell newspapers. He sponsored the catastrophic DeLong expedition to the Arctic in 1881 in which nineteen men died. He had also sponsored Henry Morton Stanley on his 1871 journey to find Scottish missionary David Livingstone in east Africa. Both projects were intended to sell papers, and they did. Given his interest in yachting, in the success of his yacht club and his desire to sell newspapers, it is predictable that the 1895 races between *Defender* and *Valkyrie III* were covered well in the press, by reporters from both the *Herald* and its rival New York papers.

In 1895, men like Bennett and their newspapers were beginning to rule the event, and newspapers went to great lengths to create heroes as a way to sell advertising and boost circulation in an intensely competitive business. In order to have heroes, they had to have villains. Lord Dunraven was unable, or unwilling, to understand that. The historical record shows that Dunraven was a brilliant, accomplished and self-disciplined man. He was a fierce competitor who deeply loved his chosen sport. However, he did not understand the game he was in off the coast of Long Island. His successor, Sir Thomas Lipton, certainly did. Lipton correctly saw the America's Cup as a potential media bonanza for his eponymous teas and made certain that he would be cast as the hero and not the villain.

Defender's Deer Isle Crew Returns to Maine

The Deer Isle crewmen were paid off and with little fanfare made their ways home. They gave no interviews, told no stories and hardly left a trace in New York; they weren't asked to. The men from Deer Isle who had helped assemble, paint, rig, clean and power *Defender*—who had saved its topmast and rig from certain catastrophe both during the trials and finals, left almost no record behind in New York.

They did hold their private celebrations, however. After most of the crew had been paid off, they presented Captain Haff a gold Masonic pin and First Mate John Allen with a meerschaum pipe. C. Oliver Iselin came alongside *Defender* and with the entire crew and officers assembled gave them a thank-you speech telling the Deer Islers that he believed that they were the best crew that ever had handled a yacht. But that was all the glory New York gave to them.

On Deer Isle, the public attention was completely and understandably different. Expectations of the heroes' return ran at a fever pitch. Reporters from the *Boston Globe, Portland Press* and *Rockland Star* were on hand. The following appeared in the *Deer Isle Gazette* on Thursday, September 26, 1895, under the blazing headline "A Rousing Reception Awaiting the Gallant *Defender* Boys":

> *Word was sent all over the Island like an electric shock last Monday afternoon* [September 23] *that twenty of the Defender's crew were in Rockland Sunday and that they were going to arrive that evening on the* [steamer] *Vinalhaven. The magnetic spark of patriotism kindled to a blaze stimulating men, women and children to the extreme. Ignorant of the change to the timetable of the Boston boats, a multitude of sightseers and participants were at the wharf when the Vinalhaven saluted Mark Island light. The band played and the cannon boomed, but the Vinalhaven sailed in as unconcerned as though nothing special should take place, and great were the expressions of dismay when no one came ashore but three Rockland drummers.*

A clarifying telegram arrived later in the day explaining the change in travel plans. On Tuesday morning, half of the *Defender* crew arrived home to their island in Maine. The *Deer Isle Gazette* reported, "Seventeen of the crew were on the steamer Mount Desert, and on her arrival, they were saluted with the screaming of whistles, roaring of cannon, shouting of friends, etc., while the Green's Landing Cadet band played 'Yankee Doodle.'" Roscoe "Ross" Fifield disembarked first and was hefted on to the shoulders of two "enthusiastic citizens" and borne through the crowd. The crew was escorted to the bandstand, where they received a welcoming speech by the Honorable E.P. Spofford, first selectman of Deer Isle. The entire group then stood on the stand and gave three cheers to the crowd for Deer Isle and the Cadet band ("and a yeller dog," according to the *Gazette* account).

Later, citizens of the island continued celebrations and admirations. Homespun poems by Deer Islers have been preserved and at the very least provide one record of who actually sailed aboard *Defender*, as well as glimpses of a more personal note of names and character. See Appendix I for one example.

George Conant had arrived home the week before. Two others had arrived the previous Friday, and twelve had remained on the payroll to help put *Defender* in winter storage. The Deer Isle crewmen were enjoying themselves at home with their friends and families, believing that their involvement with the *Defender-Valkyrie III* America's Cup races of 1895 was over. They were wrong.

Chapter 5

THE WATERLINE AFFAIR

The foul and its aftermath were only the beginning of the Dunraven fiasco of 1895. On October 25, when the cup committee released its official report to the New York Yacht Club membership, it was revealed that Lord Dunraven had privately lodged another complaint, this one not directed at the uncontrollable excursion fleet or at Haff's maneuverings prior to the second race. This complaint was far more serious. The *New York Times* reported:

> *The report of the America Cup committee, submitted to the meeting of the New York Yacht Club, says that after the first race, when Defender defeated Valkyrie on Saturday, September 7, Lord Dunraven communicated to the Cup Committee his belief that Defender had sailed the race immersed 3in. or 4in. more than when she was measured, and at the same time, his lordship stated that he believed the change to have been made without the knowledge of the owners but that it must be corrected or he would discontinue racing.*

The report hit the sporting world like a thunderclap. Lord Dunraven believed that someone or some ones aboard *Defender* were surreptitiously adding ballast to the yacht after it had been measured, thereby illegally extending its waterline. Boats with longer waterlines (all other variables being equal) tend to be faster than those with shorter waterlines in accordance with basic principles of hydrodynamics. If *Defender* were to be immersed an additional three or four inches, its waterline length, Dunraven estimated, would increase by three or four feet. With a longer waterline, it would be faster in a stiff breeze when sailing to windward. In his history of the America's Cup races from 1851 through 1901, Thomas Lawson (himself a competitive yachtsman, owner of the radical but unsuccessful 1901 defense candidate *Independence* and rival of Iselin's) wrote:

> *When the yachts came home that night* [September 7, 1895], *it was known to none but the regatta and cup committees of the New York Yacht Club that Lord Dunraven had made a charge bearing an imputation of fraud to Mr. Latham A. Fish, the New York Yacht Club member sailing on Defender, namely: that in his opinion, Defender sailed the race immersed three or four feet beyond length as measured on September 6th. Lord Dunraven told the America's Cup committee subsequently, "that he believed the change had been made without the knowledge of Defender's owners, but that it must be corrected or he would discontinue racing."*[28]

Given that Iselin was an owner of *Defender*, it is difficult to discern exactly whom Dunraven was accusing—Herreshoff? Haff? The crew? Herreshoff and Iselin both knew that *Defender* might be faster if it had more ballast aboard. They had openly arranged for additional ballast to be transferred from the *Hattie Palmer* the afternoon of September 6 once they had determined that *Defender*'s waterline was shorter than *Valkyrie III*'s. *Defender* was then remeasured, and its official load waterline was recorded and handicap calculated. However, Dunraven believed that more ballast had been added that night, as *Defender* sat lower in the water prior to the race the following morning. In short, Dunraven was accusing the Americans of cheating.

In response to Dunraven's letter, the committee ordered a remeasurement the following day, and no significant difference in waterline was detected. The accuser was unswayed. Dunraven believed that somehow the Americans had added and then removed ballast between the times of the two measurements—a difficult thing to do, but not impossible.

Lawson wrote that Lord Dunraven had been particularly sensitive to accurate waterline measurement: "There is reason for belief...that he [Dunraven] had been informed he had to do with an adversary not above the practice of altering the trim of vessels secretly."[29] Lawson goes on to speculate:

What had put such thoughts into Lord Dunraven's mind? According to the gossip of the fleet, some one among the Americans on the steamer City of Bridgeport, Valkyrie's tender, had been telling tales of alleged questionable proceedings with water ballast on a vessel formerly controlled by Mr. Iselin. The origin of this story has never been made clear, but as its substance was in pretty general circulation at the time among yachtsmen, nothing was more natural than that it should reach Lord Dunraven's ears, if he chose to listen to it.[30]

Having arrived home in England in early October, Dunraven felt less inhibited in what he said and to whom he said it. With an obvious swipe at the British aristocratic tradition, Jerome Brooks later wrote:

Not long thereafter, over the towers of Dunraven Castle, Wales, and Adare Manor, Ireland, storm signals were hoisted. They had been run up by Thomas Wyndham-Quin, Earl of Dunraven. His lordship had been stung by the sharp criticism directed at him chiefly in the American press, and by those Britishers who had questioned the reasons for his withdrawal from the second race.[31]

Lord Dunraven then made another massive mistake. In his official summary of the races he made to the Royal Yacht Squadron, he included his accusations of illegal ballasting aboard *Defender*. The report was published. To make matters worse, in an article written by Dunraven in the November 9, 1895 London *Field*, he made the same accusations. This time, he pointed his finger at the crew, who he had seen working late into the night of September 6 and dark hours of the morning of September 7 shifting ballast between *Hattie Palmer* and *Defender*. At this point, C. Oliver Iselin and the New York Yacht Club had had enough. Brooks wrote:

When the news of the Earl's charges reached the States, there was a chain reaction of violent protest. Most of the members of the New York Yacht Club expressed healthy anger and thought that Dunraven should be expelled forthwith from honorary membership.[32]

The details of what transpired are well treated elsewhere, particularly in the works of Lawson and Brooks. The culmination of the accusations and counter-accusations was a late December inquisition organized by the club to examine every aspect of Dunraven's ballast charges. The proceedings were published by the New York Yacht Club in a heavy tome in 1896.

A blue-ribbon panel of unassailable reputation presided. The dignitaries were Captain Alfred Thayer Mahan of the U.S. Navy, then sitting president of the Naval War College in Newport, Rhode Island, and an authority on naval history and strategy; J. Pierpont Morgan; Edward J. Phelps (chairman); William C. Whitney; and George L. Rives. Dunraven was represented by George R. Askwith, a prominent admiralty barrister, and Iselin by Joseph Hodges Choate, who was one of New York's leading lawyers and who from 1899 to 1905 would serve as the American Ambassador to Great Britain. Both sides were taking the inquiry very seriously.

Earlier in the month, Iselin had offered that he, Hank Haff, members of the *Defender* officer corps and all of the crew would be made available to the club to answer questions if necessary. Given that most of the men were 450 miles away on Deer Isle, this was a brave offer. Only Rollie Staples and a handful of Deer Isle men had stayed in Rhode Island to prepare *Defender* for winter storage.

In the second week of December, Iselin dispatched Staples (and probably Haff, although no correspondence concerning his trip is available) to Deer Isle on a mission. Staples's job was to take word that Iselin needed the crewmen's help. Staples brought with him blank affidavits for the men to sign, testifying that they hadn't witnessed any unreported removal or stowage of lead ballast aboard *Defender* during the night of September 6, 1895, as Dunraven had accused. In addition, if he was able, Staples was to get the Deer Islers to return to New York, during Christmas, to give in-person testimony to that effect. The results of Staples's mission are shown in Appendix IV. Fifteen men showed up, and many others agreed to be present by affidavit.

The proceedings began on Friday, December 27, with statements and testimony, including that of Lord Dunraven, who had crossed the Atlantic to press his case. Askwith also brought with him affidavits from watch officer William Henry Green of Wivenhoe, who had seen lights and "heard knocking" aboard *Defender* between two o'clock and four o'clock on the morning of September 7. William Ruffell of Brightlingsea (four miles downriver from Wivenhoe) had signed an affidavit stating that he had seen lights aboard *Defender* late in the night of September 6. Dunraven's afterguard, which consisted of Arthur Herbert Glennie, Edward Sycamore and Captain William Wardley Cranfield, also submitted affidavits stating that they had witnessed unusual activity aboard *Defender* late in the night of September 6 and early morning of September 7. Exactly what was going on, however, they could not tell.

On Monday, December 30, fifteen Deer Isle officers and crewmen were present in New York to give testimony. The proceedings of this extraordinary event show that each of the fifteen answered promptly, competently and with consistency. The transcript suggests that they were neither intimidated nor impressed. They had given up their Christmas holidays to come back to help defend the reputations of their bosses. This was testament to their character and to the loyalty they had for Hank Haff and C. Oliver Iselin.

Thirteen other men were either not asked or were unable to make the trip to New York and provided testimony by affidavit alone. When asked if whether by in-person or affidavit testimony the entire Deer Isle crew had been present, Choate answered, "Yes." He was not correct. Seven men had neither come to New York nor had provided affidavits: Bently Barbour, Ross Fifield, William Hardy, Montie Haskell, Johnnie Marshall, Charles Porter and Billie Scott. What would they have said if asked about the goings-on aboard *Defender* during the night of September 6, 1895?

The proceedings came to a bilious end on December 31. To no one's surprise, the committee found in favor of Iselin and the *Defender* crew. It could find no evidence that ballast had illegally and secretly been added to *Defender*, despite what Lord Dunraven and other witnesses had said.

The New York Yacht Club membership had had enough of the crusty Lord Dunraven. It met in closed session, and a motion was offered to rescind Dunraven's honorary membership. The prospect of the motion had reached Dunraven's ears, and in anticipation, he cabled that he hoped that the club would withhold a vote on the motion until it had received a letter from him that he'd recently drafted. The club complied, and on February 28, 1896, at 7:10 p.m., the New York Yacht Club opened and read the resignation letter from the Fourth Earl of Dunraven. The letter is shown in its entirety on the pages that follow.

The *Defender* "Waterline Affair" lives on. While researching this book, the author made several visits to Deer Isle and to the archives of the Deer Isle–Stonington Historical Society (DISHS). The DISHS has collected a number of artifacts from the 1895 and 1899 America's Cup era, important elements within the society's wonderful collection. Within that archive is a 1974 taped interview of Edmund Wood, who died the following year at the age of ninety-five.

Ed Wood was the last surviving member of the Deer Isle America's Cup teams, having sailed in *Columbia* in 1899. He went back and sailed aboard *Constitution* in its unsuccessful bid to defend in 1901. The interview covered a range of topics, including one that bears directly on the veracity of the

Recd
Friday Feb 28th
at 7.15 P.m.

27, NORFOLK STREET,
PARK LANE. W.

February 1896

To the Secretary of the New York
Yacht Club,
67 Madison Avenue
New York.

Dear Sir;

In supplement of my
cablegram and letter of the 14th
February I wish to emphasise
the fact that my letters to Mr.
Rives and Mr Phelps were written
and despatched before I heard of
the motion made by Captain
Ledyard.

The Earl of Dunraven's resignation letter dated February 28, 1896, and addressed to the New York Yacht Club. Dunraven resigned when he heard that the membership was considering a motion for his dismissal. The club's decision to dismiss an honorary member was highly unusual. This ended the nasty *Defender* waterline affair that had culminated in December 1895. *Courtesy of the New York Yacht Club.*

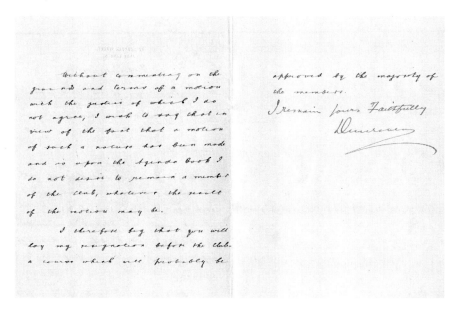

The Earl of Dunraven's resignation letter dated February 28, 1896 (pages 2 and 3). *Courtesy of the New York Yacht Club.*

blue-ribbon panel's findings in 1895. When asked about his experience aboard *Columbia*, four years after the *Defender* races, Ed Wood (E) said to interviewer Gerald Brace (GB):

> *E: But there was something on her that nobody knew about but me and my buddy—a hollow rudder.*

> *GB: Hollow?*

> *E: We had a hollow rudder, and it had a tube in it and had a pump down there so that you could pump it up just like a bicycle tire.*

> *GB: I can't understand about that rudder. You put compressed air in the rudder?*

> *E: Yes, that rudder expanded out just like a balloon. That was equal to every man's heft on that boat.*

> *GB: What was it made of?*

E: It was made of brass, just like a copper tank.

GB: How did it expand?

E: You pumped air into it, just like a bicycle tire, made the brass expand, then you let the air out and it'd all come back to the same place. She had a keel twelve feet long, all lead. The front part of her was just like a whale's head.

Ed Wood was no engineer; he was a fisherman and capable hand aboard sailing yachts. His description of the mechanics of what later became usual on large Herreshoff boats is flawed. However, what is of interest is the revelation that aboard *Columbia*, a Herreshoff and Iselin creation, water ballast was being used in the rudder. And more importantly, Ed Wood had been instructed to mention this fact to no one. A larger excerpt of his interview is shown in Appendix V.

It wasn't until 1903 that the use of water ballast technology on these big cutters was publicly announced. It was considered a great innovation at the time. Nathanael Herreshoff's son and successor L. Francis Herreshoff wrote in his book *Captain Nat Herreshoff*:

> *"Reliance"...had an ingenious rudder and steering gear. The rudder was plated of thin bronze sheets over a frame, but at its lower part, there was a small hole which let water in or out of its interior. Her rudder post was hollow, or had a hole through it, so that by having a valve at the head of the rudder post air could be forced down into the hollow rudder blade with a foot pump similar to the ones used to inflate pneumatic tires. With this arrangement, the water could be forced out of the rudder or let in as occasion required. If she steered hard, water was let into the rudder blade so its weight relieved the steering; but if she had a tendency to bear off, then more air was forced into the blade.*[33]

L. Francis was describing an innovation aboard *Reliance* that Ed Wood admitted he had secretly been manning four years earlier aboard *Columbia*. The interesting question is whether such water ballasting was going on even earlier—perhaps aboard *Defender*? Jerome Brooks wrote:

> *For some years after the Dunraven affair, the topic could be depended upon to inspire violent argument. Perhaps the most vicious incident of the aftermath*

A portrait of Edmund Wood in his later years. Wood was a member of the *Columbia* and *Constitution* crews. In a 1974 interview, ninety-five-year-old Wood recalled pumping air into the *Columbia* rudder to change its buoyancy. He was instructed to tell no one about this early innovation. *Courtesy of the Deer Isle–Stonington Historical Society. Photograph by the author.*

period was the publication of a pamphlet, "Which Was Right?" in 1898. Its author used a pseudonym, Captain J.G. Johnston. In it, an attempt was made to prove that Defender was a "trick boat," so constructed that, by means of tanks effectually hidden from the view of even an expert and pipes leading thereto and a pump attachment, water ballast to the amount of 23,870 pounds or about 11 tons could be introduced or taken out at will.

Brooks correctly dismisses this fanciful reconstruction of *Defender*'s systems. He points out that representatives from the New York Yacht Club, accompanied by Askwith himself, inspected *Defender* in winter storage prior to the late December proceedings. They found no secret tanks or compartments.

The Hart Nautical Collection at MIT in Cambridge, Massachusetts, holds most of the surviving drawings of Nathanael Herreshoff's boats. The author, along with noted marine architect Chuck Paine, reviewed the line drawings of *Defender, Columbia* and *Reliance*, paying particular attention to rudder and steering system details. All three had hollow rudders. All three had hollow rudderposts through which pneumatic air lines could run. All had valves on the bottom of the rudder to allow for water drainage when the vessel was on the ways, or while afloat if sufficient air pressure forced it out. None of the drawings show a pneumatic or pump system that would explain what Ed Wood was doing on *Columbia* or what L. Francis Herreshoff described as the great innovation in *Reliance*. What the drawings do permit is a calculation of the amount of additional weight each boat would have taken on if the rudder were flooded. In addition, they enable an estimate of the trim effect such added weight would cause. A cursory analysis shows that there would not have been enough weight added by flooding the *Defender* rudder, as Ed Wood had done aboard *Columbia* four years later, to account for the three or four inches of additional draft seen by Lord Dunraven and the other British witnesses. The *Defender* rudder simply was not large enough. Furthermore, the rudders on all three boats were positioned aft of the vessels' centers of buoyancy. In settled water, the vessels would all sit lower by the stern if their rudders were flooded. This is not what Dunraven claimed he'd seen.

However, the drawings also permit rough calculations of what additional weight would result from flooding *Defender*'s hollow keel with salt water. The answer is approximately eleven tons, a figure corroborated by Herreshoff himself, who had been asked by Iselin to estimate the weight added if the keel were flooded to within five feet of the boat's cabin sole. The weight would also be added directly under the boat's center of buoyancy, and given the narrowness and depth of the keel relative to the beam of the boat, a flooded keel would have improved *Defender*'s stiffness in a good breeze.

The boat is long gone (*Defender* was broken up in 1901, having suffered terribly from galvanic corrosion), and all eyewitnesses have long since died. And because the Herreshoff drawings omit design elements that even L. Francis Herreshoff described with certainty, we shall never know whether Lord Dunraven was right. However, we do know that Nathanael Herreshoff's masterpiece *Reliance* was using water ballast in its rudder as a trimming mechanism and that it was considered a technological innovation in 1903. Furthermore, we know that Deer Isler Ed Wood was flooding and clearing water from the *Columbia* rudder in 1899 and was clearly instructed to tell no one about it. Finally, we know that *Defender* was a leaky boat. The designs do show a bilge pump pipe that ran, as one would expect, to the lowermost point of the boat's hollow keel. Perhaps the wily Hank Haff simply allowed *Defender*'s leaks to run if circumstances permitted and he thought added weight was desirable. If so, it would have effectively taken on water ballast—not into its rudder but into its enormous nineteen-foot-deep keel. And exactly as they had testified, his men would not have been adding

A letter from Nathanael Herreshoff to C. Oliver Iselin dated December 21, 1895 (page 1). In this letter, Herreshoff gives Iselin estimates of the effects on *Defender*'s waterline and trim from flooding the keel or shifting certain numbers of crewmen around her decks. The New York Yacht Club insisted that *Defender* might have appeared to sit lower in the water on September 7, 1895, because the Deer Isle crew was crowding one side of the yacht to catch a glimpse of Lord Dunraven, the British nobleman. *Courtesy of the New York Yacht Club.*

at hand and can accomplish as much by actual trial in half an hour as I could in a days work by calculations.

For the amount of change of trim your care to get data, it would be just about proportional to the number of men used, So if you took a half doz men, and get the amount of change when placed in any desired position you can calculate easily the no require for 1 - 2 or 3 inches. In the light condition that Defender is now in I should judge 6 men would change fore & aft trim as much as seven would when in racing trim, and and 10 men would heel her as much as 11 when in racing trim. For a guess I should say, to change her trim one inch would take 9 men on her bow- and 6 men on bowsprit

Very truly yours—

Nath'l G. Herreshoff.

Herreshoff letter dated December 21, 1895 (page 2). *Courtesy of the New York Yacht Club.*

A letter from Nathanael Herreshoff to C. Oliver Iselin dated December 22, 1895. In this letter, Herreshoff clarifies the amount of weight required to increase *Defender*'s waterline length from 88.45 feet to 89 feet. His estimate of 5,800 pounds was considerably more than the amount of lead openly added to *Defender* during measurement procedures on September 6, 1895, before the first race with *Valkyrie III*. *Courtesy of the New York Yacht Club.*

ballast under such conditions. They simply did not pump the bilge. *Defender* was measured at approximately 4:00 p.m. on September 6 and sat light and dry. But twenty hours later, at noon on September 7 when the first race got underway, perhaps it wasn't as light—or as dry. If its keel were near full, it'd be four inches down and four feet longer on the waterline. The bilges were then pumped, and by the time it was remeasured on September 8, it was light and dry again.

Whether a flooded keel made it faster in light air we cannot say. But regardless of whether it worked on the racecourse, Dunraven was absolutely convinced that *Defender* sat lower in the water on race day, and it is very possible he was right.

Chapter 6

COLUMBIA, 1899

Victory and the End of an Era

On August 6, 1898, the New York Yacht Club received a cable from the Royal Ulster Yacht Club of Belfast, Ireland. This cable marked the start of a remarkable and wonderful era in America's Cup history and quite possibly saved the event from expiring under the burden of the Dunraven affairs. The cable heralded the beginning of the Lipton era.

Sir Thomas Lipton was an enormously wealthy Irishman who had made his fortune first by inventing modern food merchandising and then by backward integrating the cultivation and production of one of his most profitable items—tea. Lipton controlled his tea supply chain back to plantations he created on the island of Ceylon (today the nation of Sri Lanka). By controlling the production, quality, shipment, distribution and branding of his tea, Sir Thomas became the primary satisfier of the western world's growing thirst for this beverage.

Lipton had learned the rudiments of his prodigious commerce skills while living and working in the United States. As a teenager, he had witnessed the success and failures of retail establishments in the rapidly growing and cutthroat competitive arena of the immediate post–Civil War American market. When he returned to England at age nineteen, he applied those lessons to the more stodgy London culture, and when he redesigned his father's small market with bright lighting, open aisles and better product selections, he attracted customers. Then, with an almost Yankee doggedness and thrift, he built his business by prudently opening new stores while refining his approach. By the time he was twenty-one, Thomas Lipton owned twenty "Lipton's" grocery stores. The chain grew from there.

In 1898, Lipton was still a young man but well on his way to becoming the iconic figure known to history. He had been knighted for his philanthropy, had befriended the Prince of Wales (a competitive sailor) and was a master of publicity and indirect advertising. When asked, he always maintained that his efforts to win the America's Cup with his five *Shamrock* yachts, running from 1899 through his last challenge in 1930, were not advertising schemes. However, Lipton's persona, including the impeccable sportsmanship and infectious goodwill he always displayed while challenging for the cup, were advertisement enough. Unlike Lord Dunraven, Lipton completely understood what these glamorous big-boat races off of New York were. In fact, as the consummately honorable competitor and five-time cup loser, Lipton would help define the essence of the America's Cup. He helped contribute to its mystique more than anyone before or since. He was the affable bachelor hero that newspapers and their readers imagined should be competing for the world's most coveted sports prize.

Fearing that no respectable club would ever again challenge after the Dunraven mess, the New York Yacht Club received the Royal Ulster cable with delight. Arrangements were made, a date was set and C. Oliver Iselin was again tapped to manage the design, construction, equipping, manning and campaigning of a new defense yacht.

Building *Columbia*

Iselin was again able to retain the Herreshoff Manufacturing Company to supply the boat. *Columbia* would be longer than *Defender* on deck, although its waterline was the same. On deck, *Columbia* measured 131 feet and 8 inches, nearly 8 feet longer overall than its predecessor. Its frames were steel, topsides aluminum and underbody bronze. Herreshoff again rigged his boat with a steel mast. It was an incremental improvement over *Defender* in many ways, but overall, the two boats were similar. Herreshoff figured that what had worked in 1895 would probably work again in 1899.

Columbia was, however, much more expensive. Both Nathanael and company president John Brown Herreshoff knew they had a good thing going with the New Yorkers and their need for a fast boat. In addition, correspondence shows that Herreshoff felt that the company had lost money on *Defender*. The contract for the new boat reflected both the dynamics of

The graceful *Columbia* under sail in the summer of 1899. *Courtesy of Deer Isle–Stonington Historical Society.*

supply and demand and the Herreshoffs' need to turn a profit. While the contract price for *Defender* had been $75,000 fully equipped, the price tag for the new boat was three and a half times as much—over $250,000.

However, Iselin had little to worry about when it came to money. J.P. Morgan was commodore of the New York Yacht Club and had the year prior donated a $200,000 lot on West Forty-Fourth Street on which the club would build its marvelous new clubhouse, an architectural wonder whose façade evokes the sterns of a squadron of galleons. Morgan was among the most powerful and wealthy men in the world, and he was not about to allow the Royal Ulster Yacht Club and Sir Thomas Lipton to win the America's Cup.

Columbia was designed and constructed under the strictest secrecy. Even when it came time to launch, it was done under the cover of darkness on June 10, 1899. But despite the late hour, the press was there. Desperate to catch an image of the new yacht's underbody, one news photographer overcharged his flash pan, and the apparatus exploded. On June 11, 1899, the *New York Times* reported:

Columbia in dry dock at Erie Basin in Brooklyn, New York, October 1899. The Deer Isle crew is aboard and at work. *Image © Mystic Seaport, #1951.14.240.*

The launching was perfect in all its arrangements and was marred only by an accident caused by the wild eagerness of a photographer to get a flash-light picture. In exploding a huge charge of magnesium, he blew the legs off a boy named Napoleon Sans-Souci and seriously burned another boy, Luke

Callan, both of Bristol. The former died from his injuries. The incident was unknown to the mass of spectators.

Iselin's accounts for the 1899 *Columbia* campaign show that on June 14, 1899, twenty-five dollars was given to charity for the "boy killed at launching [in] Bristol." This was a tragic and inauspicious start to *Columbia's* magical racing career.

Iselin Again Calls for a Deer Isle Crew

Iselin had decided to hire the dynamic and younger Charlie Barr to man the new defense boat. While it was a bitter disappointment for Hank Haff, there was no dispute. On October 21, 1898, Barr wrote to Iselin at "All View" in New Rochelle agreeing to Iselin's terms of employment. He would "have charge of the new boat unless you find that I do not handle her in a capable way." He went on to write that he needed to "have control of the crew and the authority to discharge any of them for cause." Barr was to be salaried at $2,500 per annum through December 1899 and would receive a bonus of $1,000 if the cup was retained. No glory or patriotism here—just pure business.

That autumn, Iselin wrote to his old friend Captain Fred Weed. Early in 1899, Weed wrote the following letter to Iselin:

Dear Sir:

I have a list of over one hundred applications for the defender, and to secure the best men, I think it advisable to choose the men that are wanted soon as it will be convenient for you to let me know how many are wanted and how many quartermasters have you decided to have.

Hoping you have decided to take two crews from Deer Isle, I have just written Capt. Haff sending list of old crew asking him to cross out the non desirables and to mark best for quartermaster. Deer Isle appreciates your preference and hopes to see the crews of her best men in the fight for the preference to defend the cup.

Very truly yours,
F.P. Weed

By early February, recruiting was well underway on Deer Isle. In a letter dated January 23, Iselin outlined the characteristics of the new crew he desired. In these letters, a number of deficiencies of the 1895 crew are revealed. On February 8, 1899, Weed wrote back to Iselin:

Dear Sir:

Yours of Jan 23ʳᵈ duly received and contents noted. I have engaged 2nd Mate, 4 quartermasters and 32 men, nearly all of them between the age of 21 and 33, and a better crew in every respect than the one of 1895. They have shipped with the understanding that if one of them is seen going out or in a liquor saloon or known to have a drink or liquor on board or on shore that he is to be discharged at once. Also that there will be less liberty on shore than in 1895. Will you kindly send me the agreement and I will have them sign it and return to you. The 2nd Mate was with you in '95 and I think will be a better officer than the one of '95. His wages to be $50 per month, $10 extra and $5 for every race won. I have put in a few good sailor men that understand splicing and fitting wire rigging and all other riggers work. They may come in handy, as it is not always convenient to stop for riggers.

If you wish, I will have them measured for their clothes and send measurements on. If you wish me to do so, I will ship the cook or cooks that do the men's cooking. I think it would be a great saving to you in provisions. You spoke to me about Gardy [sic] Green, a man that will not keep sober. I will not send or recommend to anyone.

Very truly yours,
F.P. Weed

Evidently, during their visit to New York in 1895, at least a few Deer Islers, including quartermaster Gardie Green, had overly enjoyed their leaves ashore. Weed, perhaps tongue-in-cheek, was also offering sailors with rigging skills, knowing full well how handy they would have been aboard *Defender* during the second race of 1895 when *Valkyrie III* hooked its shroud and the crew had to jury rig the topmast.

By April 1899, the crew was ready to go. Weed had sent Ross Fifield ahead, telling Iselin that he would have sent him sooner if Fifield hadn't been twelve miles offshore in his fishing boat when word had been received that he was needed in Bristol. On February 10, Weed wrote to Iselin asking for a travel advance of $6.50 per man, a total of $247.00 for the thirty-eight

A Deer Isler in *Columbia*'s shrouds. Deer Isle crewmen occasionally "skylarked" in the rigging of their big cutters for fun, but usually their trips aloft were for more serious purposes. This and many of the on-board photographs from *Columbia* are attributable to Hope Goddard Iselin, who carried a Brownie camera aboard in 1899. *Image © Mystic Seaport, #1951.14.47.*

men he was about to send west. The new and apparently improved Deer Isle crew was ready to go.

During this back and forth between New York and Deer Isle, there is no evidence that anyone from the defense management (including Charlie Barr) ever visited Deer Isle. There are three probable reasons. First, with all of their foibles, the Deer Islers had proven their worth as America's Cup sailors in 1895. Second, the relationship between Weed and Iselin was good. They could communicate effectively by letter, Iselin trusted Weed's judgment and in addition, Hank Haff could help in a consultancy role. Third and perhaps most important, Charlie Barr was not Hank Haff. Haff was a sailor's man. He grew up sailing a workboat and never forgot his humble beginnings. He liked the men, and the men liked him. Charlie Barr was another sort of animal. As close to a full-time professional racing sailor as had been seen up to that date, he was an intense, distant and commanding presence. In all likelihood, Barr had decided that a time-consuming trip to Deer Isle was not necessary. As shall be seen, Barr's personality and methods did not wear well with the sailors from downeast Maine.

THE *COLUMBIA-DEFENDER* TRIAL RACES

After *Columbia* had spent only two weeks in the water, the New York *Sun* ran a front-page article on June 26 headlined "Columbia Shows Speed." The papers were covering the initial trials between *Columbia* and *Defender*, brought out of semi-retirement to give the new boat a workout. Although Barr and Iselin were aboard, Nathanael Herreshoff helmed *Columbia*, since the syndicate had not yet taken delivery of the new boat. Uriah Rhodes captained *Defender*. Both sailed under mainsail, jib and staysail alone. The upper topsails were not set. Under a reduced but equivalent set of sails, it appeared that Herreshoff's incremental improvements had yielded a faster boat. It also seemed to point closer to the wind.

That summer, Iselin hosted the trial races between *Columbia*, with Charlie Barr in command, and *Defender*, with Uriah Rhodes in command, at "All View" in New Rochelle. What a glorious sight it must have been for Ollie, Hope, their three children and the many neighbors and club mates who came to watch the two cutters spar. *Columbia* was consistently outperforming *Defender*, and under Barr's iron-fisted command, the Deer Isle crew again began to gel as a racing team.

However, the trials were not without incident. On July 7, William Elmer Hardy was hospitalized in Newport, and Iselin paid ten dollars for his care. On July 8, when returning to its mooring after an afternoon of racing, *Columbia* hooked the end of *Defender*'s boom with its topmast shroud. In a reversal of fortune, ironically recalling the foul between *Defender* and *Valkyrie III*, the topmast shroud held but *Defender*'s boom was bent beyond repair. It had to ship a new boom before continuing the trials.

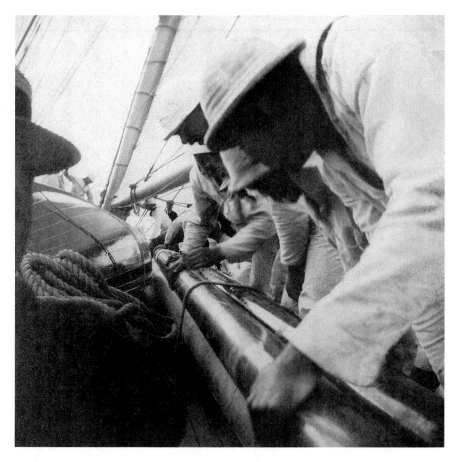

The Deer Isle mastmen readying a spar on deck. The crews were divided into groups, each under the command of a quartermaster, with specific duties on deck, on the bowsprit and aloft. *Image © Mystic Seaport, #1951.14.250.*

Over the course of the summer, the two yachts would meet many times. The final trial races were held in late August off of Newport. *Columbia* defeated *Defender* on most occasions, and its superiority was proven to the point that the Deer Isle men on *Columbia* had begun to refer to their old flagship as the "Trailer."

Above: Both *Columbia* and *Defender* had rigging problems during sea trials and trial races. Here, Herreshoff (left), Barr (center) and possibly Deer Isle quartermaster Charlie Scott (right) survey the mast. This is from a sequence of photos taken when the *Columbia* mast broke during trial races. *Image © Mystic Seaport, #1951.14.129.*

Opposite, top: *Defender* (left) leads *Columbia* in a trial race off Newport, Rhode Island, in the summer of 1899. *Columbia* regularly beat *Defender*, and the Deer Isle crew aboard *Columbia* had nicknamed *Defender* the "Trailer" by the end of the trial races. *Image © Mystic Seaport, Rosenfeld Collection, #Y402. Photographer: Charles Edwin Bolles.*

Opposite, bottom: The *Columbia* crew sheeting home a foresail as it attempts to pass *Defender* to windward in July 1899. Passing to windward would blanket the opponent. *Columbia* could sail closer to the wind than *Defender* due to the many incremental improvements made by Herreshoff in both hull and sails. *Image © Mystic Seaport, #1951.14.57.*

Columbia leading *Defender* in August 1899. Charlie Barr is at the helm while the Deer Isle men focus on their trimming work. *Image © Mystic Seaport, #1951.14.94.*

On September 5, 1899, the New York Yacht Club sent the following letter to C. Oliver Iselin:

> *Dear Sir:*
>
> *I have the honor to inform you that at a meeting of the committee on the challenge of the Royal Ulster Yacht Club, held on the Flagship* [Corsair], *off Newport, on the 4th inst., the following resolution was passed: "Resolved, that the secretary notify Mr. Iselin that, subject to unforeseen contingencies, the Columbia has been selected as the defender of the Cup under the challenge of the Royal Ulster Yacht Club."*

Herreshoff and Iselin's newest yacht, proven faster and better handled than the old *Defender*, was on its way to meet Sir Thomas Lipton and the first of his five *Shamrocks*, which had been built and launched at almost the same time as *Columbia*. Designed by William Fife Jr. and built at the Thornycroft yard on the Thames estuary near Wivenhoe, its dimensions were nearly identical to those of *Columbia*, as both were what became known as "extreme" cutters. Fife had learned from Herreshoff and constructed *Shamrock* from composite metals. It had steel frames, aluminum topsides and a bronze underbody. *Columbia* and *Shamrock* were as closely matched as any yachts yet destined for the America's Cup.

Under the command of Captain Archibald "Archie" Hogarth, on Friday, August 4, 1899, *Shamrock* departed Glasgow, Scotland, under a cut-down ketch rig for the Atlantic crossing. It was accompanied by Lipton's steam yacht *Erin*. The two vessels arrived in New York on August 20. Lipton did not make the crossing aboard *Erin* but rather steamed over on the passenger liner *Campania*, which arrived in New York a few days later.

When he had settled in, Lipton sent a warm note to Iselin in reply to the latter's welcome letter. Lipton was all grace and warmth, praising the "courtesy of your club and of those in authority in your port." The Lipton charm was already at work.

THE FIRST RACE: MONDAY, OCTOBER 16, 1899

The first race of the 1899 America's Cup was scheduled for October 3. The New York Yacht Club had decided to shift the races to October in hopes that the frustrating light September winds of 1895 would be avoided. It was not to be. Beginning on the third and then on seven more occasions after, the officers and Deer Isle crewmen were rousted from their bunks, stowed their gear aboard the *Columbia* tender *St. Michaels*, made ready the sails and handled the towline to the course start off Sandy Hook only to be met with disappointment. Four times it was due to insufficient wind, and four times because of impenetrable fog. Jerome Brooks wrote, "Betting on the races had become feverish, and stakes were high. It was said that everyone concerned with the planned races lived for nearly two weeks on chewed fingernails only."

Close maneuvering with *Shamrock*, October 1899. *Columbia* and *Shamrock* engaged in pre-start maneuvering under shortened sail. Once the warning gun sounded, however, the foresails were broken out, and these glorious racing vessels were fully underway. *Image © Mystic Seaport, #1951.14.256.*

Finally, on October 16, there was enough breeze and just enough visibility to have a race. The committee set a thirty-mile triangular course starting at the Sandy Hook lightship. The wind was out of the southeast at about eight knots, so the first leg to windward would be sailed to the south. The excursion fleet was very small due to the continuing marginal weather and the number of false alarms that had preceded the actual race day. Lord Dunraven would have been pleased. And he would have been doubly pleased, as Congress had passed a special act in 1896 prohibiting observer vessels from interfering with yacht races in American waters. The act released government vessels to

In this fantastic photograph taken during pre-start maneuvers in October 1899, *Shamrock* is seen ranging up under *Columbia*'s port quarter. The Deer Isle crewmen and afterguard are watching it closely. The American and British crews could hear the shouted orders from each other's skippers and officers. *Image © Mystic Seaport, #1951.14.297.*

help the New York Yacht Club enforce a clear racecourse. Several excursion vessel skippers had their captain licenses revoked or suspended under the authority of the act during the 1899 Cup races. The club and the authorities didn't want another Dunraven fiasco.

The starting gun sounded at 11:00 a.m. *Shamrock* crossed first and *Columbia* three seconds later, both on starboard tack. In pre-start maneuvering, however, Barr had established *Columbia* to the windward of Hogarth and his *Shamrock*. *Columbia* immediately began to show its remarkable speed. It drew ahead of *Shamrock*, and when both boats came about smartly onto the port tack, *Columbia* was clearly ahead. Barr and his Deer Isle crew were in command of the race.

Columbia gradually drew away from *Shamrock*. By the end of the thirty-mile course, Herreshoff and Iselin's new cutter crossed the finish line over ten minutes ahead of their British rival.

THE SECOND RACE: THURSDAY, OCTOBER 19, 1899

Fife and Hogarth knew that they were up against a fast boat and crew. They had to make adjustments. However, fortune was not on their side. As they practiced on October 17, *Shamrock* was hit by a puff of wind, and its topmast snapped. Of course, a spare was available, but the accident put an end to the day's workout. On Wednesday, October 18, Fife determined that *Shamrock* needed to be lower in the water and her waterline lengthened to attempt to match *Columbia*'s speed. *Shamrock* had had a handicap advantage over *Columbia* in the first race, so Fife could afford to add ballast in hopes of improving its performance. On the morning of October 18, he ordered 3,400 pounds of additional ballast aboard *Shamrock*. The boat was then towed into Erie Basin and remeasured by John Hyslop, the New York Yacht Club's official measurer. *Shamrock* was indeed lower in the water, and its waterline had increased by over one foot. Fife, Hogarth and Lipton all hoped that the result would be a faster yacht and an improved chance of catching the American flyer.

On October 19, the boats had arrived at the racecourse. In spite of the gentle breeze, pre-start jockeying was intense. It was to be a downwind initial leg, a very difficult situation from which to execute a well-timed start. The crews were working hard to keep up with their officers' orders. Each crew and helmsman watched the other closely. *Columbia* crossed the start line first, seconds after the 11:00 a.m. gun. *Shamrock* followed closely behind. In order to blanket *Columbia* and attempt to pass, Hogarth ordered the crew to set its enormous spinnaker. Within seconds, the Deer Islers on *Columbia* matched the maneuver. However, the breeze was so light that the two cutters could only creep toward the first mark, set fifteen miles away.

Due to the lack of breeze, it required nearly three and a half hours for *Columbia* to reach the mark. It started the turn at 2:24 p.m. and completed it a full minute later. *Shamrock* came past the mark five minutes behind. The two boats were then on a windward leg. *Columbia* was rewarded with a favorable wind shift that reached *Shamrock* later. But by then, the race was over. As reported by the *Sun* on October 20, 1899, "When the boats got on

In this marvelous photograph taken in July 1899, the feet of a Deer Isle crewman are just visible as he walked up a foresail sheet behind *Columbia*'s mainsail. In light air, these agile men were able to go anywhere they were needed on the vessel. *Image © Mystic Seaport, #1951.14.68.*

the same tack, which was when the *Shamrock* came about at 2:39, it was soon seen that the extra ballast put into the challenger on Wednesday was like a boomerang to her. As the seadogs put, it the 3,300 pounds of pig lead simply anchored her."

Until time expired, the remainder of the windward race was an exercise in headsail changes. As the breeze shifted, freshened and again died, both crews were kept busy as their skippers tried different combinations of jibs and staysails in an effort, in the case of *Columbia*, to finish the course before time expired or, in the case of *Shamrock*, to catch the leader. Neither succeeded.

Columbia was well ahead when the maximum allowable time of five hours and thirty minutes passed but was still two miles from the finish.

Possibly due to the large number of false starts and long delays in the regatta, when asked, Lipton consented to having the results of the truncated race stand. It was a remarkable display of sportsmanship. Unlike Dunraven, Lipton understood the value of gracious losing. This genius would endear him to the American and British publics over the next thirty years, unquestionably cementing his reputation as a great competitor and man but also helping to sell his tea.

THE THIRD RACE: FRIDAY, OCTOBER 20, 1899

Friday, October 20 dawned with a strong breeze out of the north-northwest. Finally, the heavy and humid weather pattern that had dominated the past two weeks was clearing out. Quartermasters Ross Fifield, Will Haskell, Charlie Scott and Rollie Staples, all veterans of the *Defender* races, were looking forward to the day's work. Every race that they had sailed against the British over the two campaigns had thus far been in light air. The one race during which they'd had something of a breeze, the second race against *Valkyrie III* in 1895, had been sailed with a damaged rig. They had never really been able to show the British what they were capable of in a good blow and a running sea. Today was the day. The wind was strong, and the seas were high.

Bunks and bedding were stowed aboard the *St. Michaels*. At about 8:30 a.m., Charlie Barr, C. Oliver Iselin, Hope Goddard Iselin and the rest of the afterguard were aboard. *Columbia* was tugging at its mooring pennant in the Horse Shoe anchorage inside Sandy Hook. It was ready to go.

At about 9:00 a.m., the foredeck crew secured *Columbia* to its tow, the mooring pennant was cast off and it was underway. *Shamrock* departed its mooring as well. Once clear of Sandy Hook's leeward shore, the crews made ready to make sail. First up were the enormous mainsails, hoisted by both throat and peak halyards. The big sails boomed in the wind, estimated by observers to be blowing at fifteen or twenty knots. The weather resembled a summer's afternoon in Penobscot Bay, where by virtue of the geography of the Gulf of Maine and the Bay of Fundy, the "smoky sou'wester" winds filled in at noon every warm day and blew up to twenty knots by 4:00 p.m. Some of the men probably were recalling that in those wind conditions it

As the start time approached, the *Columbia* crew and officers were focused on achieving the best position on *Shamrock*. Here they are positioned well behind but slightly to windward of the green cutter. If they can move up a boat length, they can blanket its wind and pass. *Image © Mystic Seaport, #1951.14.312.*

would have been a good time to have the lobster traps all hauled and the smack secured to its home mooring.

The American crew donned their yellow foulies—canvas wet-weather gear coated with rubber. They knew they'd be getting wet. Perhaps out of pride or ignorance, the British team aboard *Shamrock* elected to stay in their fair-weather whites.

At 10:30 a.m., the *Luckenbach* showed the signal for the course. It would be a two-leg race, each fifteen miles in length. The start would again be

Columbia heeling to port getting ready for the start. With their enormous sail areas, relatively narrow beams and deep fin keels, these boats would heel sharply. The crew and officers of these 1890s racing boats were often scrambling to stay aboard. All wore white rubber-soled shoes to improve their grip on the white pine decking. *Image © Mystic Seaport, #1951.14.116.*

abeam the Sandy Hook lightship. It stood on the westerly end, and the *Luckenbach* marked the east end of the line. It would be a downwind start with a southerly heading, very difficult for the big cutters in a heavy breeze. This was going to be a race that would test skipper, crew and vessel.

The pre-start maneuvering was again intense. Both Barr and Hogarth sailed under working sails only—full mainsail and jib. The crews were on the rigging, however, preparing for the dramatic downwind start. Topsails were furled and ready for deployment. Jib topsails the same. Montie Haskell, bowsprit man on *Columbia* and later a successful skipper in Penobscot Bay (sailing one of the early excursion schooners out of Rockland), was readying the outboard end of the long spinnaker pole. The seas were washing over the bowsprit and foredeck while he worked. He was glad for his boots and foulies.

At 10:45 a.m., the warning gun boomed from the *Luckenbach*. At the time, the tide was ebbing to the south, so the southerly downwind run was going to be fast. Hogarth ordered *Shamrock*'s heavy-weather topsail set, and out popped the small sail above its expansive main. He was playing it safe.

At 10:55 a.m., the final warning gun sounded. *Shamrock* and *Columbia* came roaring past the committee boat on a northeasterly heading on port tack, working themselves upwind of the line to be in position to turn. Hope Iselin was timekeeper aboard *Columbia*, as she had been on *Defender*, and called the times. Both boats came about on to starboard tack heading west, upwind of the start line.

At 11:00 a.m., the starting gun sounded, and Hogarth and Barr turned and made for the line. *Shamrock* was first across and set its spinnaker pole out to starboard as it crossed. *Columbia* was one minute and one second astern. The New York *Sun* reported on October 21:

> *Within half a minute after crossing the line, her clever Yankee sailors had her immense white side sail blooming in the wind. The Shamrock was somewhat slower in getter out her spinnaker; it had been too tightly stopped, and even the piping breeze lacked sufficient force to break it out. For several minutes, about fifteen feet of the head of the great sail was not doing duty.*

Although *Shamrock* was ahead, *Columbia* had executed a better spinnaker set, and the distance between the two began to close. But then problems developed on *Columbia*. Due to the strong breeze and the intentional lightness of its spars, the outer end of its spinnaker pole began to lift. Either they hadn't rigged one or its downhaul had parted in the near-gale wind. The *Sun* reported:

> *Struggling as they would, the Deer Islanders could not bring the boom to the horizontal again. The sheet also got away from them, and the spinnaker curved upward, balloon-like, until the foot of the sail was twenty feet above the bowsprit. It looked as if it were unattached to the ship and from a distance resembled a huge white cornucopia with the big end down painted on the sky.*

The *Columbia* foredeck team can be seen readying the spinnaker pole in October 1899. In the third race with *Shamrock*, *Columbia* sailed downwind with its crew barely controlling its spinnaker. The boat covered fifteen nautical miles in one hour and twenty minutes in one of the fastest races in America's Cup history. *Image © Mystic Seaport, #1951.14.286.*

With quick thinking, Barr ordered the spinnaker halyard eased. The head of the spinnaker moved forward off the masthead and out until it was positioned above the bow of the boat, one hundred feet above the water. Barr was not going to allow the pulling power of the sail to be lost. *Columbia* careened downwind with the spinnaker well out in front, sail and vessel barely under control.

Columbia continued to gain on *Shamrock*. The British looked over their shoulders and saw their opponent bearing down on them. Barr was trying to ease to the west side of the line to the mark to establish *Columbia* directly upwind of *Shamrock*, blanketing it and slowing it down. Hogarth ordered a change of topsail. Down came the heavy weather topsail, and out billowed a balloon topsail, a large topsail designed for downwind work in lighter wind. Down two races to none in this best of five series, Hogarth had to win or go home. The risk was worth it.

As it was closing on *Shamrock*, near-disaster struck *Columbia*. The *Sun* reported:

> *Just then, the patriots received a shock, the like of which has never been recorded in any other yacht race. The Columbia's spinnaker suddenly collapsed, probably because she was heading a little too far to the westward. It fell over the jib-stay to port, bringing the big spinnaker pole, a giant spar, "bang" against the stay. Then there was a great hustling aboard the Yankee flyer. Down came the pole again. Within half a minute...it had been dragged skyward, and again the Columbia bounded down the wind. The wind decreased a bit, and this enabled the Deer Isle sailors to get the spinnaker pole down into its proper place, the weight of the pole helping them.*

Shamrock and *Columbia* were on a record pace. They were sailing at maximum speed. Given that the boats covered fifteen miles in one hour and twenty minutes, their average speed was nearly 11.5 knots over the bottom. Excursion steamers and the committee boat *Luckenbach* could not keep up. It was a dramatic and wildly entertaining scene. The crewmen aboard, while working feverishly to keep the drum-tight spinnakers under control, must have known that they were in a race for the history books.

Columbia finally passed *Shamrock* on its port side and reached the turning mark just before the British cutter. The *Sun* described the scene:

> *All doubt as to who was ahead was dispelled at about 12:13 o'clock, when the Columbia was seen to pass to port of the green boat and head for the mark, which she luffed around, her men having quickly gathered in her spinnaker at 12:19. The Shamrock was in her wake, rounding only seventeen seconds later. The trained Deer Islanders were mighty quick in getting their ship into the wind. They trimmed sheets flat aft and headed northwest towards the Jersey beach on the starboard tack. The Shamrock's men were not quite so nimble. Her big mainsail seemed to get away from them. In order to trim it, they luffed up just after rounding, lost way somewhat, and while they were fumbling, the Yankee craft, with a bulldog grip on the wind, dashed across their course, apparently within three hundred feet of them, and bounded out on their weather bow.*

Columbia had won the downwind leg, and the Deer Islers had once again proven their worth.

Shamrock and *Columbia* had covered the fifteen nautical miles from the Sandy Hook lightship to the turn in one hour and fifteen minutes. The hard windward leg home lay ahead of them, but that too would be fast. In desperation, Hogarth initiated a tacking duel. After turning the mark, he threw *Shamrock* over to a starboard tack, heading toward the beach. Barr covered by tacking *Columbia*. He ordered as many men as possible to the windward rail to help reduce the extreme heel of the boat. Spectators could see a line of yellow-clad Deer Isle men sitting on the *Columbia* weather rail.

Barr tacked again, hoping for even more breeze farther offshore. Hogarth did not follow and elected the inshore route. At first, it seemed Hogarth was correct. There was a good breeze inshore, but the seas were less severe, and *Shamrock* seemed to make up ground on *Columbia*. As *Shamrock* worked its way north, the wind began to freshen even more. The spectators feared the boat might lose its rig or explode a sail. At one hour and forty-five minutes into the leg, *Columbia* was hit by a gust that almost laid it over. Barr luffed up while it righted itself, the crew and afterguard hanging on for dear life. The gust passed, and he put the boat back on course.

In the end, while *Shamrock* made up some time after its rounding problems, *Columbia* crossed the finish line at 2:40:00, followed by *Shamrock* at 2:45:17. *Columbia* had won a great race, and *Shamrock*, although losing three straight, had put up a great fight.

The crew and officers aboard the victorious Yankee boat were jubilant. They enjoyed the sail back to the Horseshoe. When *Shamrock* was pulled into anchorage, the two boats lined up next to each other. The Yankees from Deer Isle and the Britons from Wivenhoe and Ireland lined the rails and cheered each other. Sportsmanship had returned to the America's Cup.

The October 20, 1899 race was one for the America's Cup record books. *Columbia* had covered the thirty-mile course in three hours, thirty-eight minutes and 25 seconds. On a leeward/windward course, only the *Vigilant* had been faster when it defeated *Valkyrie II* in 1893 in a race in which it sailed a similar course in three hours, twenty-four minutes and thirty-nine seconds with Hank Haff at the wheel and George Conant of Deer Isle assisting.

Congratulations and the Aftermath

Praise for the *Columbia* crew finally found a voice in New York. The New York *Sun* reported the following about the *Columbia* crew from Deer Isle, as reported in the October 27, 1899 *Deer Isle Messenger*:

> *Not enough has been said of the Columbia's crew, the Deer Islanders. Their performance upon the Columbia is worthy of the very highest praise and is not without instruction. The Maine men are good sailors but not used to yachts or skilled in the science of racing, something in which the British have far more practice than the Americans. Yet in a single season, they mastered their duties so that they could get through them all with the promptitude and surety and finish of action that has never been surpassed. They have shown the Yankee quickness in learning how to do a thing and faculty to do it in the highest degree. They are good men to have in the country, and we wish them a pleasant winter.*

Jubilation on the island was once again high. Fred Weed himself telegraphed C. Oliver Iselin and Nathanael Herreshoff congratulating them for the *Columbia* victory over *Shamrock*:

> *Dated: Oct. 21, 1899 New Rochelle, NY*
> *To: Oliver Iselin & Nathaniel Herreshoff*
> *Yacht Columbia*
> *In the name of the citizens of Deer Isle, we congratulate you on your honorable victory over Shamrock.*
>
> *F.P. Weed, Stonington, Maine*

After each *Columbia* victory, a gun was fired in Stonington. Unfortunately, upon receiving the cable announcing the final victory on Friday, October 20, the gun was reloaded too quickly and a serious accident occurred. The *Deer Isle Gazette* reported:

> *Enthusiasm was at its height Friday when the news of the victory of the Columbia was received. The cannon was again brought out and seemed to catch the enthusiasm, for it went off prematurely, breaking Fred Beck's right arm and mangling his hand quite badly, besides filling his face with powder. Several others received injury.*

Almost immediately after the yachts had crossed the finish line off Sandy Hook, Sir Thomas Lipton announced that he would challenge again, and he did so in 1901 with his second *Shamrock*. Lipton knew a good thing when he saw it. Despite losing and, in fact, partly because he lost, he had become enormously popular in America, the world's largest consumer market. But he also was a sportsman, and he hoped he might actually win. However, after defeating *Constitution* and *Independence* in trial races, *Columbia* would defeat him once again in 1901. And it would again be commanded by Charlie Barr, but not a single Deer Isler would be aboard. The question, of course, is why?

Hank Haff understood Deer Isle and its sailors. Charlie Barr did not. Fundamentally, neither did Iselin and the New York Yacht Club. Reviewing the press reports and historical records suggest that after the great 1899 victory, three things happened that together severed Deer Isle's connection with the America's Cup. First, in 1901, Hank Haff was pulled out of retirement and at the age of sixty-three took command of *Independence*, a radical new boat designed by William Crowninshield and owned by Thomas Lawson of Boston. Haff attracted five Deer Islers to his crew. But Lawson's bid to defend the cup was unsuccessful, and Haff never sailed in an America's campaign again. Second, Iselin and the New York Yacht Club commissioned Herreshoff to build a new boat. The *Constitution* was intended to succeed the *Columbia*, but under the command of Uriah Rhodes, it could not beat Charlie Barr in the rejuvenated *Columbia*. After a difficult start to his relationship with Deer Isle, Rhodes attracted twenty-three loyal Deer Islers (including George Conant and twelve other Deer Isle America's Cup veterans) to crew *Constitution*. Third and most important, Deer Isle had had enough of Captain Charlie Barr. During the long wait for the start of the series against *Shamrock*, friction between crew and skipper had begun to bubble to the surface. Perhaps unfairly, press reports suggested that the Deer Islers had difficulty meeting Barr's exacting standards. Barr went on to greater success in yacht racing than anyone before or since, partly due to the high expectations he set for his crews and for himself. Reports suggested that the Deer Islers grated under his demands. These same reports also suggested that the men from downeast Maine had a problem with Barr's immigrant origins. They were a Yankee crew sailing a Yankee-designed, Yankee-built and Yankee-owned boat helmed by an immigrant Scot. These reports may or may not have been accurate. They were written at a time when patriotism ran very high as the Spanish-American War was drawing to a close. However, there may be a kernel of truth in both accounts.

An article in *Down East* magazine in the 1950s told a more cogent although incomplete story of why *Columbia* in 1899 was Deer Isle's last America's Cup defense:

> *In 1902, when Hank Haff was appointed skipper of the huge Boston-owned sloop Independence, he let it be known that he wanted a Deer Isle crew and appointed Fred Weed to select the men. Meanwhile, in February of that year, Uriah Rhodes, captain of the new Constitution...and already favorite for the Cup defense selection, arrived at Deer Isle with a list of forty-five racing hands he wished to interview. From these, twenty would be selected to add to others already chosen. Rhodes was a distinguished racing skipper, but his proposed screening upset many of the islanders. On top of this, he ignored Fred Weed and, as a result, left the island without having signed a single hand from a possible 200 men who had all pledged to Fred Weed that they would not sign papers until Hank Haff had picked his crew of about forty men. The unforeseen consequence of the action against Rhodes was that the Deer Isle men weakened their racing connections and lost the favor of other captains.*[34]

Independent sources confirm that Rhodes arrived on Deer Isle in January 1901 and failed to recruit his crew. He blamed it on a bad snowstorm that inhibited his ability to get around the island. However, by March 15, 1899, the *Deer Isle Messenger* announced that "through the courtesy of Mr. Geo. Conant, who has been acting for Captain Rhodes in the selection of the crew from the Herreshoff cup defender," twenty-three Deer Islers had, in fact, signed on to man the new Iselin boat. Perhaps out of the need for work or their sense that they were signing on with a winner, these men, including Conant, raced against their old friend and skipper Hank Haff, who commanded *Independence* and the five Deer Islers he had aboard. None went back to sail with Barr. Charlie Barr went on to dominate competitive sailing until the hiatus of World War I, but he never again had much to do with Deer Isle and its humble heroes—the men who had helped him win his first and probably greatest America's Cup victory.

DEER ISLE SAILOR POETRY

Courtesy of Herreshoff Museum, Bristol, Rhode Island

THE DEFENDER: WINNER OF THE AMERICAN CUP IN 1895
By Captain Walter Scott

Sit down with me old timers, those of you alive,
Who made a name for your native town back in '95;
When C. Oliver Islin [sic] told Hank Haff, "I'm badly in need,
I'm sending you to Green's Landing with a message to Capt. Fred Weed."

Says Hank to Fred, "Here I am, now what am I going to do?
Mr. Islin has built the Defender and badly needs a crew.
I talked with Mr. Islin and he listened for a while,
He wants a crew and none will do except they're from Deer Isle."

Capt. Haff knew very well his efforts would succeed,
As he chose Deer Isle's ablest man when he selected Capt. Weed.
Capt. Weed combed the Island's best and told them what to do,
And put them in line as members of the old Defender's crew.

These men proved as able as crew as ever sailed the sea,
They gave this Island an honor list that will go down in history.
When in that race an order was given to slack or trim a sheet,
Before Mate Allen could open his mouth, those boys were on their feet.

A mastheadman's job on that fine ship was no easy place,
When you're up aloft over a hundred feet, with her rail down in a race.
A man aloft in this man's place has no value for his neck,
Should the mast let go, there's a hundred feet between him and the deck.

No Marconi sails or Genoa jibs around her masts did curl,
But real he-man sails of canvas that took a man to furl.
With the Defender's Crew and her rail down, carrying all she could lug,
How could John Bull ever expect to take away the mug?

Look near and far and give Hank Haff another Deer Isle crew,
Put them against the boats today and see what they would do.
They would keep the "mug" right here at home as sure as you're alive,
They'd give John Bull the same surprise he got in '95.

DEER ISLE AMERICA'S CUP CREWS

The following tables show the names and positions of the Deer Isle men who served aboard an America's Cup yacht either as the defender chosen by the New York Yacht Club (*Defender* and *Columbia*). These lists do not include earlier yachts (such as *Vigilant*), aboard which Deer Isle men served either as officers or as American hands within a predominantly Scandinavian crew.

Each of these names and positions is supported by a minimum of two independent sources validating inclusion. As is the case with this entire book, the author welcomes corrections to these tables and the basis for such correction.

Defender (1895)

Given Name	Family Name	Position	Age as of 12/15/1895	Later Served on *Columbia*?
Bently	Barbour	Quartermaster	25	No
Irving G.	Barbour	Quartermaster	27 (est.)	No
Charles	Barter	Seaman	27	Yes
John E.	Billings	Quartermaster	24	Yes
Herbert	Bray	Seaman	24	Yes
Samuel	Bray	Seaman	27	Yes
Warren	Bray	Seaman	35	No
George	Conant	Second Mate	34 (est.)	No

Given Name	Family Name	Position	Age as of 12/15/1895	Later Served on *Columbia*?
Horace ("Harsee")	Davis	Seaman	50	No
Walter ("Coo")	Eaton	Seaman	20	No
Roswell ("Ross")	Fifield	Seaman	22	Yes
Harry W. ("Winslow")	Gray	Seaman	23	No
Gardner ("Gardie")	Greene	Quartermaster	Unknown	No
Elmer E.	Hamblen	Seaman	33	No
William E. ("Elmer")	Hardy	Messboy	34	No
Eben	Haskell	Seaman	22	No
Ernest C.	Haskell	Seaman	26	Yes
Montaford ("Montie")	Haskell	Seaman	21	Yes
Willard ("Will")	Haskell	Masthead man	21	Yes
Thomas	Horton	Seaman	30	No
John ("Johnnie")	Marshall	Lazarette man	32	Yes
Floreston ("Forrest")	McCauley	Seaman	24	Yes
Winslow ("Willie")	Pickering	Seaman	32	No
Charles	Porter	Seaman	Uknown	No
John	Pressey	Seaman	35	No
James ("Jim")	Robbins	Bowsprit man	22	No
Thomas ("Tommie")	Robbins	Seaman	27	No
Charles ("Charlie")	Scott	Masthead man	35	Yes
William ("Billie")	Scott	Seaman	32	Yes
Stephen	Sellers	Seaman	34	No

Given Name	Family Name	Position	Age as of 12/15/1895	Later Served on *Columbia*?
Roland	Small	Seaman	29	No
John	Staples	Quartermaster	26	No
Rollins ("Rollie")	Staples	Seaman	31	Yes
George	Stinson	Seaman	27	Yes
Leslie	Stinson	Seaman	23	No

Total number of Deer Isle men serving on *Defender* team: 35
Total serving on both *Defender* and *Columbia* teams: 14

Columbia (1899)

Given Name	Family Name	Position
Charles	Barter	Seaman
John	Billings	Seaman
Charles	Bray	Seaman
Herbert	Bray	Seaman
Samuel	Bray	Seaman
Edward	Carman	Seaman
Alva	Conary	Seaman
William ("Win")	Conary	Seaman
F.M.	Conley	Seaman
John	Eaton	Seaman
William	Ellis	Seaman
Roswell ("Ross")	Fifield	Quartermaster
Arthur	Gray	Seaman
Charles	Gray	Seaman
Leslie (Lester)	Gray	Seaman
Lyman	Gray	Seaman
Edward	Greenlaw	Seaman

Given Name	Family Name	Position
Alonzo	Gross	Seaman
Jason	Gross	Seaman
John	Gross	Seaman
Daniel	Hall	Seaman
Ernest	Haskell	Seaman
Judson	Haskell	Seaman
Montaford ("Montie")	Haskell	Seaman
Philip	Haskell	Seaman
Willard ("Will")	Haskell	Quartermaster
Nathan	Low(e)	Seaman
John ("Johnnie")	Marshall	Lazarette man
Floreston ("Forrest")	McCauley	Seaman
Alfred	Pettee	Seaman
Arthur	Powers	Seaman
Andrew	Scott	Seaman
Charles ("Charlie")	Scott	Quartermaster
Rollins ("Rollie")	Staples	Quartermaster
George	Stinson	Seaman
Augustus	Thompson	Seaman
Cyrus	Thompson	Seaman
Everett	Thompson	Seaman
Nelson	Thompson	Seaman
Theodore	Thompson	Seaman
Edward ("Ed")	Wood	Seaman
Arthur	Young	Seaman
Will	Young	Seaman

Total number of Deer Isle men serving on *Columbia* team: 43

Appendix III

DEER ISLE MEN IN 1901 TRIAL HORSES

Constitution

Given Name	**Family Name**	**Prior America's Cup Experience**
Charles	Barter	*Defender* and *Columbia*
John	Billings	*Defender* and *Columbia*
Edward	Carman	*Columbia*
George	Conant	*Mayflower, Vigilant, Volunteer, Defender*
Clarence	Dow	None
Winfield	Dow	None
Fred	Eaton	None
Jeremiah	Eaton	None
John	Eaton	*Columbia*
Thomas	Eaton	None
Charles	Gray	*Columbia*
Gardner ("Gardie")	Green	*Defender*
Montaford ("Montie")	Haskell	*Defender* and *Columbia*
Belcher	Howard	None
Fred	Joyce	None

APPENDIX III

Given Name	Family Name	Prior America's Cup Experience
William	Morey	None
James ("Jim")	Robbins	*Defender*
E. L.	Saunders	None
Fred	Smith	None
Cyrus	Thompson	*Columbia*
Marsh	Thompson	None
Theodore	Thompson	*Columbia*
Edward ("Ed")	Wood	*Columbia*

Total number Deer Isle men on *Constitution* team: 23
Total with prior America's Cup experience: 12

Independence

Given Name	Family Name	Prior America's Cup Experience
Charles	Bray	*Columbia*
Walter ("Coo")	Eaton	*Defender*
Alvah	Emerson	None
Floreston ("Forrest")	McCauley	*Defender* and *Columbia*
Arthur	Young	*Columbia*

Total number of Deer Isle men on *Independence* team: 5
Total with prior America's Cup experience: 4
Total serving in one or more America's Cup competitor 1895–1901: 76

DEER ISLE CREWMEN AND THE DUNRAVEN INQUISITION

Given Name	Family Name	Position	New York Testimony
Bently	Barbour	Quartermaster	None
Irving G.	Barbour	Quartermaster	In person
Charles	Barter	Seaman	Affidavit
John E.	Billings	Quartermawster	In person
Herbert	Bray	Seaman	Affidavit
Samuel	Bray	Seaman	Affidavit
Warren	Bray	Seaman	Affidavit
George	Conant	Second Mate	In person
Horace ("Harsee")	Davis	Seaman	Affidavit and in person
Walter ("Coo")	Eaton	Seaman	Affidavit
Roswell ("Ross")	Fifield	Seaman	None
Harry W. ("Warren")	Gray	Seaman	Affidavit
Gardner ("Gardie")	Greene	Quartermaster	In person
Elmer E.	Hamblen	Seaman	Affidavit and in person
William E.	Hardy	Messboy	None
Eben	Haskell	Seaman	Affidavit
Ernest C.	Haskell	Seaman	Affidavit

Given Name	Family Name	Position	New York Testimony
Montaford ("Montie")	Haskell	Seaman	None
Willard ("Will")	Haskell	Masthead man	Affidavit and in person
Thomas	Horton	Seaman	Affidavit and in person
John ("Johnnie")	Marshall	Lazarette man	None
Floreston ("Forrest")	McCauley	Seaman	Affidavit
Winslow ("Willie")	Pickering	Seaman	Affidavit and in person
Charles	Porter	Seaman	None
John	Pressey	Seaman	Affidavit and in person
James ("Jim")	Robbins	Bowsprit man	Affidavit and in person
Thomas ("Tommie")	Robbins	Seaman	Affidavit
Charles ("Charlie")	Scott	Masthead man	Affidavit and in person
William ("Billie")	Scott	Seaman	None
Stephen	Sellers	Seaman	Affidavit and in person
Roland	Small	Seaman	Affidavit
John	Staples	Quartermaster	In person
Rollins ("Rollie")	Staples	Seaman	Affidavit
George	Stinson	Seaman	Affidavit and in person
Leslie	Stinson	Seaman	Affidavit

Total number of Deer Isle men who testified in New York on December 27, 1895: 15
Total who testified by affidavit only: 13
Total who did not testify in the Dunraven affair: 7

Affidavit Signed by Rollie Staples
Courtesy of the New York Yacht Club

I, Rollins Staples, being duly sworn, depose and say that I am thirty-one years of age and reside in Deer Isle, in the State of Maine, and was one of the crew of the yacht *Defender* during the America's Cup races in September 1895. During the first week of September, the *Defender* went to New Rochelle, were her cabin fixtures, water-tank and ice-tank out and about forty-two pigs of lead put in her hold. On September 6th, the *Defender* was towed to Erie Basin, where more lead was put on board before she was measured and placed upon her cabin floor. Late in the afternoon, we were towed to Sandy Hook. On the way down, I went to bed and fell asleep before we reached Sandy Hook. I was awakened by the noise made by the crew in cutting and stowing the said lead, which had been taken on board, at Erie Basin. The noise ceased about ten o'clock, after which I went to sleep. After the race on September 7th, the *Defender* was towed to Bay Ridge, where the *Palmer* came alongside and the men had their supper and transferred their bedding to the *Defender*, after which the *Palmer* went away and, as I verily believe, did not again come alongside until after six o'clock the next morning. I was on board the *Defender* or the *Hattie Palmer* at all times between the time when the *Defender* was measured on September 6th and the time she was re-measured on September 8th, and I do not know of any lead or other ballast having been put in or taken out of the *Defender* during such time except the said lead so taken on board at Erie Basin, as aforesaid, and which was, as I am informed and believe, transferred to the *Hattie Palmer*, and there cut and passed back to the *Defender* during the evening of September 6th, and I verily believe that no other lead or ballast was put in or taken out of the *Defender* during such period. I slept during the nights of September 6th and 7th in the forecastle of the *Defender*, and I heard no noises such as would be made by putting in or taking out ballast except as herein mentioned.

Rollins Staples
Sworn to before me this 14th Day of December 1895
Elmer P. Spofford, Notary Public

Appendix V

ED WOOD INTERVIEW

In 1971, two members of the Deer Isle–Stonington Historical Society interviewed ninety-four-year-old Edmund Wood, the last surviving member of the *Columbia* crew. It is a wide-ranging and entertaining conversation with a downeast islander, and the following excerpts highlight his experiences aboard *Columbia*, including his role pumping air, or admitting water, into *Columbia*'s rudder. Wood was interviewed on September 9, 1971, by Gerald Brace (GB) and Helen McKay (H). The interview was taped by Floyd Markham.

> *GB: Did the Columbia come before the Defender?*
>
> *E: No, the Defender came first. She was a Herreshoff boat.*
>
> *GB: She carried a club topsail, I suppose.*
>
> *E: Yes.*
>
> *GB: How did you handle it?*
>
> *E: Oh, boy. Everything was like a feather to those boys. Nothing was heavy.*
>
> *GB: The club topsail was pretty heavy though, wasn't it? I always wondered why it worked. I would think you'd get it all fouled up.*

E: The only time we got it fouled up was in the last race. We were at Sandy Hook in the Highlands. It was blowing forty miles per hour—a northeaster.

GB: Did you carry full sail?

E: We put the spinnaker on her and the Shamrock the same. The Shamrock went right out past us a mile or more before we got our spinnaker broke down so it took ahold. It was fifteen miles from where we started to the down course to come back again. We got that old spinnaker down where she belonged and old [illegible] begun to come. When we went passed that stake buoy at fifteen miles, our boat was at the stern of the Shamrock, and the Shamrock boys were all hollering. We were going like lightning. We tacked right around that old buoy and came back again. By the time they finally got straightened up, we were on our course a mile ahead of them. It was just one hour and forty seconds from the time we passed that stake buoy until we crossed the finish line. Fifteen miles on the home run…that was traveling. Seems as though the harder it blowed, the better the boat liked it. She seemed to work right up like a thoroughbred horse. You couldn't help but notice it. And everybody laid there with their head under the rail—a four-inch rail. You had to have your head under it.

GB: Who was your captain?

E: Captain Charlie Barr.

GB: Oh, yes. He was a famous man.

GB: Was he a Yankee man, Charlie Barr?

E: No, he was Scotch. We'd be laying down on the deck, and he'd start to walk forward and you'd swear he had snowshoes on. He had the biggest feet I ever see on any man.

GB: Didn't he sail the schooner Atlantic across when she made her record run?

E: I don't know. All I knew was when he was captain of the Columbia, I was the smallest man on board there. All the rest of them were 6'2" or 6'4" and weighed 200 or more, but I only weighed 148 pounds.

GB: Tell us about the first time you were on the Columbia and they needed someone to climb the mast.

E: When I went on board her, the deck was covered with people. Mr. and Mrs. Herreshoff were there…their guests and the whole crew and a lot of other people. You could hardly see the deck at all. She was lying alongside Herreshoff's wharf. When I came on board, one of the officers came along and said, "Mr. Wood? Mr. Gray? Come along with me." So we went and changed into white ducks. When I walked past the mate and another man, they were consulting together, and I thought then something was wrong. So I came up on the deck and went up to where the masthead man was and said, "It can't be done. You'd have to heist me up 160 feet as far as you can go in the bos'un's chair, and 6 or 7 feet above that there's nothing. Now, the topmost ball must be varnished. That's what what Mrs. Iselin wants." The mate turned to me and said, "Ed, do you think you can varnish that topmost ball?" We knew each other when we were boys at the harbor. The masthead man pipes up and says, "You can't shin it." The mate says, "Do you want to try it, Ed?" I said, "I'll do my duty."

So I got into that bos'un's chair, and the mate fastened me in and the varnish alongside. The board wasn't very wide. You get in and put your feet in and sit down and up you go. I went up seems as though a hundred miles—up through swamps and everything else. So many lines, you know, crossing those spreaders. I looked up at the darn thing, and I had a funny feeling come over me. How am I going to shin that darn topmast with a varnish brush with varnish in it? You couldn't take the pail with you. I dipped the varnish brush into the varnish and wiped it on both sides and stuck it between my teeth and off into the bos'un's chair and up I went up that darn mast. I locked my feet though and put my hands around. I varnished that thing round and round, and I looked down and the people looked about two feet high. Then they let me down, and I didn't know but I'd have to stop it. I could have stopped it by grabbing a rope bit. I let her come and I struck the deck with a wallop. The mate grabbed the brush and the varnish. The man who was tending the lines for me said, "I was never so scared in my life."

GB: But weren't you scared?

E: Scared? No, I didn't have sense enough…I never worked for a better man in my life than Charlie Barr. I want to tell you about unloading the stuff. We got to the boat, and Mr. and Mrs. Iselin were up on the deck. I mistrusted something. As soon as the man hollered "All fast," I grabbed a barrel of sweet potatoes and gave it a throw and it landed way up on the deck. Then I threw up 100 pounds of potatoes and 125 pounds of beef. Old Barr came around the deck and said, "Wood, come up here and get your breakfast." I said, "I have the groceries to unload." Barr said, "Other people can do it." When I was sitting there eating breakfast, Mrs. Iselin came in and put her hand on my shoulder and said, "What's your name?" "Edmund C. Wood." I said. "Little boy Ed—strongest boy on earth," she said. She called me that for the next six months every time she saw me.

GB: How long did the crew work together and practice before the actual race?

E: About five months and a half.

GB: Did you have winches for the sheets?

E: But there was something on her that nobody knew about but me and my buddy: a hollow rudder.

GB: Hollow?

E: We had a hollow rudder, and it had a tube in it and a pump down there so that you could pump it up just like a bicycle tire. The British crews came aboard, and we showed them around. I was lucky. I got the one that was young and could speak English. Most of them couldn't speak English.

H: What was their nationality?

E: They were all Englishmen.

H: But they couldn't speak English? What did they speak?

E: Why, they spoke English, but we couldn't.

H: You spoke Yankee?

E: Yes. We were old Yanks.

GB: I can't understand that about the rudder. You put compressed air in the rudder?

E: Yes. That rudder expanded out just like a balloon that was equal to every man's heft on that boat.

GB: What was it made of?

E: It was made of brass, just like a copper tank.

GB: How did it expand?

E: You pumped air into it just like a bicycle tire...made the brass expand. Then you let the air out, and it'd all come back to the same place. She had a keel twelve feet long, all lead. The front part of her was just like a whale's head. Sir Thomas Lipton was the owner of Shamrock, one of the nicest men anyone ever met in the world. I was in the locker splicing wire rigging me and my buddy. He came down on the wharf where we were working and I says, "Oh, Mr. England, I'm glad to meet you." He says, "You're one of the boys on the Columbia." I said, "You haven't got a job for me on your boat, have you?" He says, "If you want it." He came in where we were splicing. I gave him a nickel keg to sit on—that's the best I had. "Want to have a bottle with us?" So he had a bottle of beer with us.

ENDNOTES

Chapter 1

1. New York *Sun*, 1899.
2. Brooks, *The $30,000,000 Cup*, 62.
3. Ibid., 117.

Chapter 2

4. Churchill, *Maine Communities*, 12.
5. Leamon, *Revolution Downeast*, 82.
6. Ibid., 155.
7. Ibid., 221.
8. *Deer Isle Messenger*, May 1, 1900.
9. Butler, *Story of Wivenhoe*, 48
10. Ibid., 56.
11. Ibid., 131
12. Ibid., 157
13. Ibid., 158
14. Ibid.

Chapter 3

15. Brooks, *The $30,000,000 Cup*, 124.

16. The *Sun*, June 11, 1899.
17. Lawson and Thompson, *Lawson History*, 157.
18. Herreshoff, *Capt. Nat Herreschoff*, 186.

Chapter 4

19. Bray and Pinheiro, *Herreshoff of Bristol*, 57.
20. In 1898, as it became clear that the New York Yacht Club again needed Herreshoff, the company produced an estimate of what the price for *Defender* should have been. Needless to say, the number was considerably higher than the actual price—$98,000 as opposed to the contracted price of $75,000. This reworking of the numbers included modifications that had been made after *Defender* had been delivered to its new owners in June 1895, as well as the addition of a "fair profit" for the Herreshoff Company. Evidently, Herreshoff was conveying that they had enjoyed no profit on the *Defender* contract.
21. Lawson and Thompson, *Lawson History*, 161.
22. Ibid.
23. Brooks, *The $30,000,000 Cup*, 125.
24. Ibid., 126.
25. Lawson and Thompson, *Lawson History*, 159.
26. Ibid., 160.
27. Brooks, *The $30,000,000 Cup*, 128.

Chapter 5

28. Lawson and Thompson, *Lawson History*, 166.
29. Ibid., 164.
30. Ibid.
31. Brooks, *The $30,000,000 Cup*, 135.
32. Ibid., 137.
33. Herreshoff, *Capt. Nat Herreschoff*, 234.

Chapter 6

34. *Down East* magazine, n.d., p. 29. Courtesy of Deer Isle–Stonington Historical Society.

BIBLIOGRAPHY

Aldrich, James M. *Centennial: A Century of Island Newspapers*. Stonington, ME: Penobscot Books, 1985.

Beken of Cowes. *The America's Cup: 1851 to the Present Day*. London: The Harvill Press, 1990.

Bicentennial Committee of Deer Isle, Maine. *Deer Isle Remembered: 1789–1989*. Stonington, ME: Penobscot Bay Press, 1989.

Bray, Maynard, and Carlton Pinheiro. *Herreshoff of Bristol: A Photographic History of America's Greatest Yacht and Boat Builders*. Brooklin, ME: WoodenBoat Publications, 1989.

Brooks, Jerome E. *The $30,000,000 Cup: The Stormy History of the Defense of the America's Cup*. New York: Simon and Schuster, 1958.

Burchard, R.B. "The Cup Defenders and Their Crews." *Outing*. September, 1895.

Butler, Nicholas. *The Story of Wivenhoe*. Wivenhoe, UK: Quentin, 1989.

Churchill, Edwin A. *Maine Communities and the War for Independence*. Augusta: Maine State Museum, 1976.

D'Antonio, Michael. *A Full Cup*. New York: Penguin Group, 2010.

Dietz, Lew. "The Skipper Goes Ashore." *Downeast,* June 1956.

Hatch, Louis Clinton. *Maine: A History*. New York: The American Historical Society, 1919. Reprinted in 1974 by New Hampshire Publishing Company.

Haviland, William. Various articles published in the *Island Ad-Vantages*, Stonington, Maine. Also, in-person interview conducted in Deer Isle, Maine, June 2012.

Herreshoff, L. Francis. *Capt. Nat Herreshoff: The Wizard of Bristol*. White Plains, NY: Sheridan House, 1953.

Hosmer, George L. *An Historical Sketch of the Town of Deer Isle Maine*. Sunset, Maine: Deer Isle–Stonington Historical Society, 2001.

Kenealy, Captain A.J. *Yachting Wrinkles: A Practical and Historic Handbook of Valuable Information for the Racing and Cruising Yachtsman*. New York: Outing Publishing Company, 1899.

Lawson, Thomas W., and Winfield M. Thompson. *The Lawson History of the America's Cup: A Record of Fifty Years*. Boston: Winfield M. Thompson, 1902.

Leamon, James S. *Revolution Downeast: The War for American Independence in Maine*. Amherst: The University of Massachusetts Press, 1993.

Maine Department of Marine Resources. www.maine.gov/dmr/commercialfishing/recentlandings.htm.

The New York Yacht Club. *Report of the Special Committee of the New York Yacht Club on Certain Charges Made by the Earl of Dunraven*. New York: Douglas Taylor Co., 1896.

Paine, Charles. Naval architect. Interview conducted in Tenants Harbor, Maine, July, 2012.

Pastore, Christopher. *Temple to The Wind: The Story of America's Greatest Naval Architect and His Masterpiece, Reliance*. Guilford, CT: The Lyons Press, 2005.

Rousmaniere, John. *America's Cup Book: 1851–1983*. Dallas, TX: Taylor Publishing Company, 1983.

———. "Henry Coleman Haff (1837–1906)." Presentation by John Rousmaniere at America's Cup Induction Ceremony, Newport, Rhode Island, June 10, 2004.

Rowe, William Hutchinson. *The Maritime History of Maine: Three Centuries of Shipbuilding & Seafaring*. New York: W.W. Norton & Company Inc., 1948.

Russell, Charles. "The 'America' Cup Race." *The North American Review*, September, 1899.

Simpson, Richard V. *America's Cup: Trials and Triumphs*. Charleston, SC: The History Press, 2010.

Spectre, Peter H., and Benjamin Mendlowitz. *A Passage in Time: Along the Coast of Maine by Schooner*. New York: W.W. Norton & Company, 1991.

United States Commissioner of Navigation, Department of the Treasury. *Annual Report*, 1899.

INDEX

ABOUT THE AUTHOR

Mark J. Gabrielson is a U.S. Coast Guard–licensed master and a trustee of the Marion–Bermuda Cruising Yacht Race. He is a graduate of Princeton University and after more than three decades in business is now a graduate student at Harvard University, in extension, concentrating in history. He also serves as a research intern at the Naval War College in Newport, Rhode Island. He is a New Englander, dividing his time among Ridgefield, Connecticut; Boston, Massachusetts; and Deer Isle. This is his first book.